The Daniel Fast
A Devotional

Nannette Elkins

Copyright © 2014 Nannette Elkins

All rights reserved. This book, or any portion thereof, may not be reproduced without the express written permission of the publisher except for the use of brief quotations in a book review.
ISBN-13: 978-1503236264

Unless otherwise identified, all Scripture quotations are taken from The Holy Bible: King James Version.

DEDICATION

To the Lord Jesus Christ, I am humbled and thankful for the inspiration You have given me for this first book. May many learn to fall in love with You through fasting and prayer.

For Douglas, thank you for encouraging me to write and to put myself out there. Without your belief in me, and God's gentle nudging, Hope in the Healing would never have brought about this devotional. Your unconditional love and support for this book made me believe dreams really can come true.

For Jenna, my last minute lifesaver and Randa who held my hand through this journey. I am grateful.

CONTENTS

Preface 7

Introduction 8

Foreword 9

God Will Restore: Introduction to Fasting Part 1 10

God Is Awake: Introduction to Fasting Part 2 17

Why Fasting? 22

Here We Go! 28

As Unto the Lord 34

From the First Day 38

Desperate Times, Desperate Measures 42

Bind the Strong Man 47

Rebuilding the Walls 51

To Open Their Eyes 55

Not by Bread Alone 59

When Others Intercede 62

Chosen, Committed & Commissioned 66

Jonah: And God Saw 70

Cornelius: There is More! 75

Except Ye Abide 83

The Good, The Bad & The Ugly 89

The Battle is Not Yours, But God's 95

Looking for the Redemption 99
Face to Face 104
For All the Right Reasons 108
Ebenezer, the Lord Has Helped Us 112
Ezra: By the Good Hand of God 117
Lives Were Changed; Prayers Were Answered 122

PREFACE

The Daniel Fast has been a part of my life for several years now and yet I do not consider myself an expert on the subject. In 2013 I felt led to write a few posts about it for my blog, Hope in the Healing. The response was overwhelming, and before I knew it, I was blogging every single day in January to help those that were attempting the fast. God amazingly gave me something to give to others the entire month.

The Bible is full of examples of fasting; some I knew about, others were a surprise to me. I studied every day and gleaned so much from the Word of God. I realized there were books available on The Daniel Fast but there was little to help someone with a daily focus.

Enter this book. With God's help, I have attempted to give you, the reader, a roadmap to follow that can be a help to you on this journey. Fasting isn't about just going without food. If done properly, it can propel you to new heights in your relationship with God. I pray you find this book a tool that you will refer to again and again as you make fasting a regular part of your spiritual life.

INTRODUCTION

The Daniel Fast has quickly become one of the most popular corporate and individual fasts among Christians worldwide. Many are seeking a closer relationship with God and have heard of the benefits of fasting for the spiritual man and the physical man. Even though there are many self-help books available that explain the Daniel Fast, there are few, if any, devotionals to take you through the normal 21 day fast.

This book gives three days of preparation before the fast; explaining the importance of fasting, the rewards and the different types of fasting. If you have questions about fasting; they will be answered in those first three days. That precious preparation time will take the reader on a spiritual journey, discovering what God will do for us when we fast and also things we are NOT to do while fasting.

For each day of the fast, there will be a devotional with an example from the Bible of fasting: what caused them to go on the fast, what happened when they did and what application we can take from it. Included at the end of each devotional are Daniel Fast-approved recipes for that day. There are also engaging images in every chapter that bring to life the subject and characters discussed.

Simple and easy to read, The Daniel Fast Devotional will help you to learn how to make the most of your fasting time by pouring yourself into the Word of God each day and making prayer a priority. Fasting without prayer is just a diet!

You will also draw closer to God, learn how to deny your flesh for spiritual purposes and become more disciplined in your walk of faith. Even more importantly, you will be in tune with what God wants to do in your life and become a conduit for His spirit. This is a journey of a lifetime that can forever be repeated and built upon.

GRAB YOUR BIBLE AND LET'S GET STARTED!

FOREWORD

Nannette Elkins has a rare gift of conversation. In her newest book, she invites you to pull up a chair and share her experiences with the Daniel Fast and her passionate pursuit of a deeper relationship with her Savior. Nannette provides a banquet of delicious, wholesome recipes interwoven with personal true stories, as well as practical tips and spiritual encouragement. Written in easy-to-understand language, Nannette's story will enable you to embark upon your own successful Daniel Fast journey, as well as experience a renewed desire for more significant encounters with God.

~RANDA M. CHANCE, SPEAKER AND AUTHOR, *OF CABBAGES AND KINGS*

1 INTRODUCTION TO FASTING PART 1
GOD WILL RESTORE

How many times do we go to bed with the worries of the day on our minds; wondering how we are going to fix all of the problems in the world?

Will the bills get paid? How long before our company shuts down? Is the cancer going to return? Will our children get back together? Is that divorce going to become final this year?

Night after night we toss and turn, trying our best not to let the sin of *worry* overtake us.

We are all guilty of it; we are human.

Lately, I had struggled with this and could not shake it. Many things were troubling me. I was trying to fix them all in my own mind but couldn't and it was getting me down. I finally decided enough was enough and in desperation I finally did something I had always wanted, and needed, to do.

I went on an extended fast.

You might say that the Bible says our fasting should be a secret. No. Jesus said when you fast to not be like the Pharisees who *want* others to *know* they are fasting. They walked around with long, drawn looks on their faces and said things like, "Woe is me! I am fasting!" They wanted to appear more holy, godlier and more spiritual than others. That is not the purpose.

However, if we do not share our experiences, how will we learn? How will we grow? How will we bless one another?

This fast was one of the hardest things I have ever done in my life but also one of the most victorious and liberating spiritual battles the Lord has ever helped me win.

His Word says some things only come about by prayer *and* fasting.

"And when he was come into the house, his disciples asked him privately, Why could we not cast him out? So he said to them, This kind can come out by nothing but prayer and fasting." Mark 9:28, 29 NKJV.

The devil was tormenting me. Satan had been whispering in my ear for way too long, and unfortunately, I had been giving him credit by believing what he was saying.

Worry is one of his most successful tactics. It rates right up there with fear. The *wringing of your hands* type of worry is his specialty. He really had me going with about three big issues at once.

But fasting puts Satan IN HIS PLACE.

The Bible says, *"Submit yourselves therefore to God, resist the devil and he will flee from you."* James 4:7 KJV.

He has to obey when you *quote* the Word, *obey* the Word and *live out* the Word!

When you add fasting into the mix, you are breaking *YOU*. You are humbling *YOU*. The chains begin to fall; he has no power left. You begin to hear God's voice, His whispers. You *understand* His Word, *feel* His power, and *trust* His promises.

The one single passage of scripture that jumped out to me while I was on this fast was the fasting message we might be familiar with in Isaiah. Finally, after all of these years, I understood what the Lord was saying here, and it is so beautiful.

First, the Word. It's a little lengthy, but stay with me. It's worth it.

'Why have we fasted,' they say, 'and You have not seen?

Why have we afflicted our souls, and You take no notice?'

'In fact, in the day of your fast you find pleasure,
And exploit all your laborers.
Indeed you fast for strife and debate,
And to strike with the fist of wickedness.
You will not fast as you do this day,
To make your voice heard on high.

Is it a fast that I have chosen,

A day for a man to afflict his soul?
Is it to bow down his head like a bulrush,
And to spread out sackcloth and ashes?
Would you call this a fast,
And an acceptable day to the Lord?

Is this not the fast that I have chosen:
To loose the bonds of wickedness,
To undo the heavy burdens,
To let the oppressed go free,
And that you break every yoke?

Is it not to share your bread with the hungry,

And that you bring to your house the poor who are cast out;
When you see the naked, that you cover him,
And not hide yourself from your own flesh?
Then your light shall break forth like the morning,
Your healing shall spring forth speedily,
And your righteousness shall go before you;
The glory of the Lord shall be your rear guard.

Then you shall call, and the Lord will answer;
You shall cry, and He will say, 'Here I am.'

If you take away the yoke from your midst,

The pointing of the finger, and speaking wickedness,
If you extend your soul to the hungry
And satisfy the afflicted soul,
Then your light shall dawn in the darkness,
And your darkness shall be as the noonday.

The LORD will guide you continually,
And satisfy your soul in drought,
And strengthen your bones;
You shall be like a watered garden,
And like a spring of water, whose waters do not fail.

Isaiah 58:3-11 NKJV.

The Jews had the proper form for their fasting, but they were messing up everything else that went with it. They were finding pleasure in their fasting time instead of using it to draw closer to God. They were *"driving hard all of their workers"*, meaning that even though on fast days there was no work done, on the day before and the day after they worked them even that much harder to make up for it.

They were quarreling and fighting, and their fasting was making them irritable with one another…a good sign they were NOT spending time with their Maker.

They were *"hiding from their own flesh"*; they were not helping their own. They were being selfish during fasting time. This is another *"Woe is me"* attitude about fasting: *avoiding helping others because you are suffering.*

Verse nine says they were oppressing one another by placing yokes, or unnecessary burdens, upon their brothers and sisters. They were also pointing fingers at each other, spreading rumors and lies about their fellow

Christians.

Again, they had the method right, but their hearts were in bad, bad shape. They were upset that the Lord had not noticed that they were in sackcloth and ashes. They had fasted, but He had not noticed.

So the Lord speaks and tells them they have it all wrong. He says, *"Is not this the fast that I have chosen?"*

And here is where I have always looked at it differently:

"To loose the bonds of wickedness, To undo the heavy burdens, To let the oppressed go free..."

We would hear this part preached and taught and get all excited that God was going to do this for us.

But look at what He says next...

"And that you break every yoke?"

That *WE* break every yoke? I thought *He* was going to do that? He can and He will, but here He says *WE* are to break every yoke!

The fast that the Lord is pleased with is when *we* loose those bonds of wickedness, undo the heavy burdens we have placed on one another, let the oppressed go free and break every yoke!

What else does He say?

We are to share our bread with the hungry, bring the poor to our house, cover the naked that have no clothing, and not ignore those that need our help. Also, stop pointing your finger and spreading vicious rumors. Those are pretty important.

That is the fast that God has chosen.

He says that when we do those things something will happen:

"Then shall thy light break forth as the morning, and thine health shall spring forth speedily: and thy righteousness shall go before thee; the glory of the Lord shall be thy reward.

Then shalt thou call, and the Lord shall answer; thou shalt cry, and he shall say, Here I am. If thou take away from the midst of thee the yoke, the putting forth of the finger, and speaking vanity;

And if thou draw out thy soul to the hungry, and satisfy the afflicted soul; then shall thy light rise in obscurity and thy darkness be as the noon day:

And the Lord shall guide thee continually, and satisfy thy soul in drought, and make fat thy bones: and thou shalt be like a watered garden, and like a spring of water, whose waters fail not.

And they that shall be of thee shall build the old waste places: thou shalt raise up the foundations of many generations; and thou shalt be called, The repairer of the breach, The restorer of paths to dwell in." Isaiah 58:8-12 KJV.

Look at all of those precious promises! Your health will spring forth, righteousness will go before you and the glory of the Lord will be your reward. If you call on the Lord, He will answer, He will always be your guide. Another version says that you will be *"known as a rebuilder of walls and a restorer of homes."*

All of this when you choose the right fast: God's fast!

When your heart is in the right place.

When you are doing it unto the Lord and not to be seen.

When you are breaking yokes and setting people free by forgiving, restoring, clothing and feeding then …

God will also restore you.

2 INTRODUCTION TO FASTING PART 2
GOD IS AWAKE!

Even the early Church fasted and prayed regularly after they received the Holy Ghost. We have a continual war going on between the carnal and the spiritual that will not end until after the Lord comes back for His people, the final battle is fought and Satan has been put in his place. Forever.

In order to be overcomers while we are living in this world, we must have a relationship with Jesus Christ and we must learn how to pray and fast to keep our bodies, our flesh, under subjection.

"Humble yourselves in the sight of the Lord and he shall lift you up." James 4:10 KJV.

Fasting will kill that inner man. You will be filled with the power of God so you may be able to overcome.

Let's explore some particulars of an extended fast before we go into the Daniel Fast. You will remember that I said I was doing an *extended nine-day fast* a few months ago for specific needs. I did not eat *ANY FOOD* at all for the entire nine day period.

However, just as you would not give an infant a sirloin steak, you must start out slowly. If you are a newcomer to fasting, simply fast a single meal the first few times, and then fast an entire day, just drinking water. This is not a game and you must be careful how you treat your body. It can be very, very dangerous if you are careless with fasting.

Whatever you choose, do NOT go without water---ever! The body cannot survive.

Do that for several weeks in a row, fasting one full day each week. Then you should be ready to move up to a two or three day fast.

There are no *rules*. Pray about it! See where the Lord would lead you. If you do set out to go on your first extended fast of ten days or more, it is wise to get support in prayer, and if you have any health issues, you will need to seek a doctor's advice. You do have to use common sense in all things.

Of course God can take care of you, but He expects you to be wise.

It is also advisable, if you have never done an extended fast before, to seek counsel from your pastor. Especially if you are young in the Lord, please go talk to the shepherd of your soul. He would love to help guide you in this area, and even more importantly, it is so good to have others praying for you during an extended fast.

I chose a partial juice and water fast. A few days into the fast I became dehydrated and did drink some Gatorade to replenish electrolytes and fluids. From the third day until the ninth day I drank some organic juice. The only reason I didn't go a full ten days was because it takes about four days to come off of an extended fast of that nature. With our frequent trips out of town and being on the road, etc., I decided to do my *winding down* at home.

During the fast, you must drink plenty of water. You will be flushing toxins from the body and the water will help keep you hydrated and the toxic waste moving on through like it should.

You may even notice some physical healing from your fast! Longer fasts of 21 to 30 days can definitely heal the body of physical ailments, but shorter fasts have been known to cleanse the human body of harmful toxins that will then heal whatever was causing the pain or disruption in the body's ability to perform or operate. Cold sores, boils, blemishes, ulcers, even more serious diseases have been healed through the benefits of fasting.

The body's ability to cleanse itself truly is a healing process which brings fantastic results.

After the first three days, it does become so much easier. You really are not that hungry if you drink enough water.

The most important thing is that you take that time that you would normally be eating and spend it PRAYING!

Praying and studying the Word, talking to the Lord and discovering things about you. Where are your issues with trust coming from?

What is causing you to worry so much?

Is there sin somewhere?

The Lord will show you things during a long fast about *YOU* that you haven't had time to notice before. You must slow down and listen.

Quarterly, a three-day or seven-day fast is a wonderful suggestion. Then once a year, those who really benefit most from fasting can try a 21-day, or even a 30-day fast. Some will add in broth or other types of simple nourishment to help strengthen when necessary, especially depending on the type of physical labor that their job requires. Again, use wisdom.

It is also good to stay away from, or at least taper off of, social media, the computer, television or anything that distracts, or keeps your mind from God during your fast.

The Spiritual Aspect.

I admit for the first part of the fast I was expecting miracles to fall out of the sky, signs and wonders to appear and all of my troubles to vanish overnight. Maybe not to that extreme, but I have heard stories of some who had been on long fasts and had deep spiritual encounters.

That wasn't necessarily my experience, but when I had finished the fast, I cannot explain to you the way that the weight of what I had been carrying began to be lifted from my shoulders. I had been living under a cloud of depression for weeks. Some of it was my own fault.

Many things had happened during my fast. A great spiritual warfare had been fought on my behalf!

When the Church is fasting, the enemy is intimidated. Satan isn't worried one bit when we are content with the status quo. But if the Church ever realizes the power it possesses through prayer and fasting, the devil would be on the run.

So it wasn't DURING the fast for me, it was AFTERWARD. I started noticing a difference in the way I prayed. I prayed with AUTHORITY. I had carried it all along, I just didn't use it. But by getting rid of my baggage, cleansing my mind and detoxing the attitudes I was carrying, I could use that God-given authority I had with boldness in the Holy Ghost!

Not only had those burdens been lifted but I could also speak to the father of lies, and say, "Get behind me, Satan!" He had to leave; I had the authority to make him go!

I also had a difference in my approach; a change in the way I looked at my problems.

Problems? I gave those to Him! I decided there was nothing, absolutely nothing I could do about those *three things* that were keeping me awake every night. I could not physically change any one of them, and they had physically consumed me, depressed and oppressed me to the point of outright despair.

Thankfully, in that moment of desperation, I found enough strength to do something that I had wanted to do my entire life, but didn't think I ever could.

Well, *I* couldn't. But I asked God to help me. You can do it too. Fasting can change your life. It will draw you closer to God, help you see things about yourself that you need to change, allow God to dig out the ugly and replace it with His grace, and lift those heavy burdens from you that you just don't need to carry or worry about any longer.

You need your sleep, friend. Let Jesus take your worries.

He's going to be up all night anyway…

3 WHY FASTING?

Many begin the Daniel Fast as a part of their New Year *resolutions*. Some churches even do it corporately, which is a wonderful thing. It is a great time to come together in unity, denying yourself certain foods, all for the purpose of renewing your walk with the Savior. You want to clean out the old and make way for the new!

Jesus also said that some things just do not come about by prayer alone.

"Then the disciples came to Jesus in private and asked, 'Why couldn't we drive it out?' And He said to them, 'Because of the littleness of your faith; for truly I say to you, if you have faith the size of a mustard seed, you will say to this mountain, 'Move from here to there,' and it will move; and nothing will be impossible to you. But this kind does not go out except by prayer and fasting.'" Matthew 17:19-21 NASB.

This was serious business. They had been with Jesus earlier and had performed many miracles with Him. They had even had prayers answered before. What was different this time?

Haven't we been there? We prayed for someone or some*thing*, and nothing happened.

What did Jesus answer and say to them? *"But this kind does not go out except by prayer and fasting."*

What kind?

One kind of thing that especially requires prayer coupled *with* fasting is that of a demonic nature, such as we see here in Matthew 17. The disciples could not *"drive it out"* and Jesus told them they needed to have fasting and prayer in order to do it.

Jesus did too!

When Jesus was led up into the wilderness, He fasted and prayed for 40 days. He was tempted by the devil but He was able to overcome because of the power of prayer and fasting. He had strengthened the inner man! *"And Jesus returned in the power of the Spirit into Galilee: and there went out a fame of him through all the region round about."* Luke 4:14 KJV.

He had returned from the wilderness after fasting for 40 days and nights and He returned *"in the power of the Spirit."*

Now, you know there is good reason to fast; but why the Daniel Fast?

In the first chapter of the Book of Daniel we read that Daniel and his three friends were put into a Babylonian training program while in exile under King Nebuchadnezzar. They did not want to defile their bodies with the rich food brought in by the kings' servants so they requested that they be given only vegetables and water for ten days. Their meat was also likely sacrificed to idols, a strict *no-no* for the Jewish people.

At the end of the ten days, they were not only well, but had also prospered physically and spiritually above all the others in the court! Daniel was appointed an advisor to the king and began to interpret his dreams.

Later on, in the tenth chapter, Daniel had a vision of a great war that caused him to mourn and fast for three weeks. This is where the *Daniel Fast* originates from. Daniel ate only plant-based foods for three weeks. That is why you see so many people, and now so many churches, starting the first of the year on a three-week Daniel Fast. They typically go without meat, dairy, sugar, breads and no artificial or processed foods. Basically they eat only fruits, vegetables and whole grains and drink only water. (And plenty of it!)

There is nothing in the Bible that commands God's people to fast as Daniel fasted but it certainly brings many benefits when done in the right spirit and for the right reasons.

Also, because you are cleansing your body of unwanted toxins you will feel so much better during those weeks and even afterward.

One word of caution: I do see an alarming trend about the Daniel Fast. Many are taking it as an opportunity to go all-out and create these fabulous vegan recipes that wow the taste buds. This is concerning because this is a FAST, not a diet or a trend.

There are already many Daniel Fast cookbooks on the market and more coming every day. It is easy to get carried away with trying to make all of your meals copycats of your *normal foods*. Be careful that it doesn't become a recipe club! Naturally, you will be trying some new things and looking at ways to fix your meals differently, but it should be simple.

Keep reminding yourself that this is a time to draw near to your Lord, not, "Can I HAVE this?" and, "Am I ALLOWED that?" You are fasting, not continually looking for ways to make your new foods taste like your regular diet. It is a time for *self-denial*, not *self-indulgence* and pleasure.

Remember, if you are just fasting and *not praying*, you are wasting your time. Yes, you might lose a little weight, but if you are doing it for that purpose you are missing the point.

If you are prone to cheating, it is good to *clean out* your pantry of anything that would tempt you before you begin. The women of Israel got rid of anything with leaven (yeast) in it when they were preparing for the Passover, and many still do it today.

Most of all, in the days leading up to the fast, no matter when you start, (and it doesn't matter when you start!), *prepare your heart!* Ask the Lord to show you things that need to be brought out into the open and dealt with, or done away with altogether. He will do just that because He loves you so much.

Your *flesh* is going to rebel during the fast, especially at the beginning. It is going to be a fight to stay away from the things that you normally put into your system every day. That is why it is so important to *PRAY and FAST together!* Keep focused on why you are doing what you are doing.

Give yourself time to prepare. It may take more time to fix a meal on the Daniel Fast since it is almost always made from scratch. There are no artificial ingredients involved here. Think ahead so you do not get caught and decide to just grab something not on the plan.

Did I mention to be sure to study and meditate on the Word during the fast?

Set aside time every day to meet with the Lord! Pray, and then pray again. He desires to meet with you, so do your best to keep at it and make time for Him. While you are denying yourself things that you enjoy, such as sweets, colas, coffees, breads, etc., remember WHY you are doing it. Don't just check off the days on the calendar. It would be such a shame to only complete 21 days of a vegan diet and not accomplish something in your spiritual walk.

You may even want to journal. If you have never been one to journal, maybe now would be a good time to write down your thoughts as you experience this unique time with God. You might be surprised how He communicates with you during your quiet time. Keep your heart, mind and Bible open.

Always remember that God will honor your sacrifice. *"And ye shall seek me, and find me, when ye shall search for me with all your heart."* Jeremiah 29:13 KJV.

The general food list for the fast is simple and basic. You may have any fruits, vegetables and WHOLE GRAINS (with no added sugar) that you want. This whole grain list includes brown rice, whole wheat pasta, plain popcorn, oats, grits, barley, etc. Oils are allowed on the Daniel Fast, just do not overdo it. Beans of all kinds are included in the fast. You may also enjoy any variety of nuts or seeds. Spices are allowed, just be sure and be careful with your salt intake.

Naturally, you will be drinking water and lots of it. Juices are allowed as long as there is no added sugar.

What you are NOT to consume is meats, dairy, anything with white flour or yeast. Sweeteners are forbidden, including artificial additives. No processed foods! Chemical additives are prohibited. You are going all-natural. No breaded and fried foods, no sweets or treats. Finally, no coffee, sodas, energy drinks, etc.

As we mentioned in Part 1, there are no hard and set rules, but these are the given guidelines that most follow when participating in the fast.

Again, not everyone does it exactly as it is written above. Some use honey as a sweetener or natural maple syrup. Others would strictly forbid it, which is just an example.

You can find some good organic products at many health and organic specialty stores. They have many ready-to-eat foods that are acceptable, such as whole grain flatbreads and tortillas, which are great for making a veggie *sandwich*. Again, READ THE LABELS!

Tomorrow you will be ready to begin The Daniel Fast. Ask the Lord to strengthen you for this exciting journey!

4 HERE WE GO!

The Daniel Fast is a Biblically-based, partial fast taken from Daniel 1 and Daniel 10 when Daniel the Prophet refrained from eating anything but vegetables (this would have included fruits, although most participants do eat them) and drank only water. It is comparable to a vegan diet with a few more restrictions. We will talk about them further at the end of the post.

Daniel was born in the kingdom of Judah in a noble household. King Nebuchadnezzar conquered Jerusalem, taking 650,000 of Daniel's countrymen into bondage, back to his Babylonian kingdom. The king decreed that all of the young and handsome princes from Judah must go into a training program to work in the king's court. Daniel was among the chosen.

They were to be fed very well, with rich meats, sweets and plenty of wine. The only problem was that the men from Judah followed the Law of Moses and did not consume many of the foods on the list! Additionally, the Babylonians' food was usually part of a sacrifice to their idols. Daniel would most definitely not have consumed food used as a sacrifice to an idol made of stone, wood or any other material. He served the One, True God, Jehovah!

Daniel asked if he and his men could abstain from the rich and pleasant food for only ten days to prove that their way of eating, only vegetables and water, was much healthier for their bodies. They agreed and at the end of the ten days? *"At the end of ten days it was seen that they were better in appearance and fatter in flesh than all the youths who ate the king's food. So the steward took away their food and the wine they were to drink, and gave them vegetables."* Daniel 1:15, 16 ESV.

Right away we see how beneficial a fast of this nature is to the body. In only ten days it was noticeable that these men were not eating rich foods! They looked better and they felt better.

For Daniel, it wasn't just about the right way to eat. He was connected to the Source as well. He served the Most High and wasn't intimidated by those around him. He fasted for the right reasons and God honored him.

You will be wasting your time if you are just cutting out meats, sweets, breads and your favorite fancy coffee but never take time to pray!

"When Daniel knew that the document had been signed, he went to his house where he had windows in his upper chamber open toward Jerusalem. He got down on his

kneesthree times a day and prayed and gave thanks before his God, as he had done previously." Daniel 6:10 ESV.

Daniel is recorded to have prayed at least three times every day, usually at the same time. It is so helpful if you can start your day with the Lord, spend some time in His Word and get strengthened for the day ahead; you are going to need it.

If you have specific things you are fasting about, whether it is your job, finances, your marriage, children, extended family, direction, healing, restoration, whatever the need, ask the Holy Spirit for guidance.

If you have offended someone, or if there is sin that needs forgiveness, repent. Take care of that at the beginning of the fast.

"If thy brother trespass against thee, rebuke him; and if he repent, forgive him. And if he trespass against thee seven times in a day, and seven times in a day turn again to thee, saying, I repent; thou shalt forgive him." Luke 17:3-4 KJV.

You will also receive strength to resist and to be able to turn from sinful habits. *"Having therefore these promises, dearly beloved, let us cleanse ourselves from all filthiness of the flesh and spirit, perfecting holiness in the fear of God."* 2 Corinthians 7:1 KJV.

Hopefully it goes without mentioning, (and in this case we aren't going totally without food), but let's go over it just for the record. We do not want to *"appear to men to fast."* Let us see what Jesus said about it:

"Moreover when ye fast, be not, as the hypocrites, of a sad countenance: for they disfigure their faces, that they may appear unto men to fast. Verily I say unto you, They have their reward. But thou, when thou fastest, anoint thine head, and wash thy face; That thou appear not unto men to fast, but unto thy Father which is in secret: and thy Father, which seeth in secret, shall reward thee openly." Matthew 6:16-18 KJV.

We can understand clearly here Jesus was saying to not walk around with your head down, pouting that you *have to fast*. The Word says, *"they have their reward"*, meaning that is all they have, recognition. They gloried in the *appearance* of fasting!

This should be something between you and God, unless of course your entire church congregation is doing it, then of course, that is a corporate fast and it is not a secret. It is also good to have a close friend praying for you during an extended fast. The purpose is to focus on Him and not bring attention to yourself.

The Lord will bless the sincere heart that seeks Him! So do it with all that is within you, every day as a sacrifice unto your God, denying yourself pleasures that you would normally enjoy. Do not try to make your new foods taste like your normal diet; otherwise it is not a sacrifice.

Remember, we are denying ourselves things that we enjoy, *so we only eat until we are satisfied.* We are not stuffing ourselves until we are sick.

RECIPES

You will enjoy your meals and you will delight in this clean, healthy way of eating. One of my favorite things to make on the Daniel Fast is homemade granola. It is so good and healthy for you that I even make it sometimes when I am not on the fast. It is easy to do and makes a good large batch that can be put in an airtight container and eaten as it is or as a cereal in the mornings with some plain almond milk. *(not vanilla or flavored almond milk that would contain sugar).*

Granola

3 cups oats
¾ cup coconut
¾ teaspoon cinnamon
½ teaspoon nutmeg
¼ teaspoon salt
½ cup coconut oil or canola oil
1 teaspoon vanilla and any kind of nuts and dried fruits desired

This recipe normally calls for up to ½ cup of raw honey but the Daniel Fast restricts honey calling it a *precious food* that Daniel would not have eaten while on his fast. Some still consume it, calling it a natural food. Others do not. I leave that up to the individual.

Mix the oats, coconut, and spices together. Grease a 9x13 pan or a sheet cake pan and add the dry ingredients. Mix the oil and vanilla (and honey if you use it) and incorporate into the granola, stirring until well mixed. Smooth out and bake at 300 degrees for about 30 minutes, stirring every 10 minutes so it doesn't burn on top. Let cool, then break up and store in an airtight container. Delicious alone or with unflavored almond or soy milk.

Add the fruit and nuts *after* the granola comes out of the oven. This is a base recipe that you can adjust to your taste.

Spinach Smoothie *(You won't taste the spinach!)*

1 ripe banana
1 cup frozen blueberries or raspberries or both!
1 cup unsweetened almond or soy milk
½ teaspoon cinnamon
½ cup fresh or frozen spinach
2–3 ice cubes

Place the banana, berries, almond milk, cinnamon, and spinach in a blender; blend until smooth. Add ice to reach desired consistency and serve cold. *Makes 1 serving.*

One of our favorite meals was a simple dish of grilled vegetables, usually zucchini and yellow squash, red onion, mushrooms, maybe some peppers. If it's too cold for the outdoor grill, cooked in a cast iron skillet with a dash of olive oil makes them delicious! Then serve it over brown rice and add a salad with vinegar and oil dressing. Paul Newman's Own has a great one that fits the fast, and you have dinner!

Remember, the Daniel Fast, or any other, is to be a sacrifice. It is a time of commitment to the Lord, a time of drawing near to Him and denying the flesh of some of its pleasures. You do not want to gorge yourself on this fast. Just enjoy a regular meal with normal-sized portions.

Make time at the beginning of your day to spend with God; you can do it! Set that alarm a few minutes early and you will not be sorry.

Meditate on the Word. Feed on the manna that comes from above and just see how rich your mind and soul will become during this time of devotion to God.

Our desire should be to know HIM.

We are not on a diet; we are striving to be more like Jesus. Paul said, *"That I may know him, and the power of his resurrection, and the fellowship of his sufferings, being made conformable unto his death..."* Philippians 3:10 KJV.

God is well pleased as you sacrifice what is pleasurable to you on a daily basis.

5 AS UNTO THE LORD

We have talked quite a bit about the WHY's of fasting.

Conclusion:

1. Fasting without prayer is just going without food.

2. Fasting to lose weight is NOT fasting, it is called a DIET.

3. Fasting just because everybody else is doing it? This is not pleasing unto the Lord.

But today, what if your pastor has asked you to fast and you don't see the importance?

Maybe the shepherd of your soul has asked your congregation to go on a fast for a certain period of time this month and you can do it however you please: going without any food, a juice fast, Daniel Fast, partial fast, a meal each day fast, etc. But again, that's just not your thing. "God hasn't laid it on my heart; but when He does I will most certainly fast then."

Or, your pastor has asked the entire congregation to do the 21-day Daniel Fast but you think that isn't really fasting. Forty days without any food, only water; now, **THAT** is fasting!

Satan would love for us to stay in the dark about the benefits of fasting!

Daniel was in a battle with the spirit world when he went on his 21 days of fasting and prayer. Satan and his cohorts resisted the angels that were to be sent for an answer to his prayers, but finally, they were able to break through. The earth began to quake and the men that were with Daniel fled because of fear! You can read of this battle in Daniel the tenth chapter.

Twenty-one days Daniel had been fasting...no *pleasant bread*, no flesh (meat) and no wine touched his lips. Basically fruits, vegetables, whole grains and only water to drink. He was humbling himself before God and denying himself things that he would normally enjoy. And when he did that, look what happened: It shook heaven and hell.

Is there power in fasting? Yes!

Does it matter if we do it or not? Yes!

The spirit world is real. Angels are working on our behalf and God wants to release power like we have never seen before in these last days. However, we must do our part. We are not going to experience it just sitting around doing nothing.

Daniel has a vision at the end of this three week fast: *"In the third year of Cyrus king of Persia a word was revealed to Daniel, who was named Belteshazzar. And the word was true, and it was a great conflict. And he understood the word and had understanding of the vision. In those days I, Daniel, was mourning for three weeks. I ate no delicacies, no meat or wine entered my mouth, nor did I anoint myself at all, for the full three weeks."* Daniel 10:1-3 ESV.

Three weeks of fasting had made Daniel very weak and he said to the angel, *"O my lord, by reason of the vision pains have come upon me, and I retain no strength. How can my lord's servant talk with my lord? For now no strength remains in me, and no breath is left in me."* Daniel 10:16, 17 ESV. The angel immediately responded.

"Again one having the appearance of a man touched me and strengthened me. And he said, 'O man greatly loved, fear not, peace be with you; be strong and of good courage.' And as he spoke to me, I was strengthened and said, 'Let my lord speak, for you have strengthened me.'" Daniel 10:18, 19 ESV.

He was strengthened over and over again in this encounter with the angels. He had finished his three week fast and was physically without strength. The Bible even says that the man in the vision told Daniel that Michael, the archangel and this other angel were fighting together in the spirit world for Daniel!

Daniel was fasting unto the Lord. Jehovah didn't turn his back on Daniel but honored his sacrifice and his commitment and sent warrior angels on his behalf.

He will do the same for you.

Fast as unto the Lord. Watch and see what will happen in your life this year when you put fasting and prayer together.

RECIPES

Smoothies are another great source of protein and fiber on the Daniel Fast. They taste good, are easy to fix and are great on-the-go. You can make up so many variations of your own.

Strawberry Banana Smoothie with Oats!

1 cup unsweetened soy or almond milk
¼ cup quick oats
2 bananas, broken into chunks
1 cup strawberries
½ teaspoon vanilla extract
2 Tablespoons apple, pineapple or orange juice

In a blender, combine soy milk, oats, banana, and strawberries. Add vanilla and enough juice for desired consistency; blend until smooth. Pour into glasses and serve cold. *Makes 2 servings.*

Fasting together...unto the Lord!

6 FROM THE FIRST DAY

Sometimes the food on the Daniel Fast is so good we can forget we are fasting, and that can pose a problem. We are to eat a simple meal until we are comfortably full and get up and walk away.

But what about *snacking*? Is it allowed?

Three small meals a day and two moderate snacks would seem reasonable for the fast. (Actually, that would seem reasonable for any normal diet!) It wouldn't make sense to eat all day long just because you are on a different kind of fast. You are still supposed to be denying yourself pleasures and sacrificing things that the flesh would normally enjoy in order to give yourself to prayer and the Word.

If we are continually eating throughout the day, just because we can, we would be missing the purpose of the fast.

There needs to be sacrifice.

When you fast at other times, and go without food, you spend that time that you would normally be eating in prayer, right? When on the Daniel Fast we should look for opportunities to spend time with the Lord. Maybe in the evenings you could change your normal routine for the duration of the fast.

If you usually spend that time watching television, playing games on the internet, iPad, etc., perhaps you could cut back on those hours and spend some of that time in prayer. Shut everything down an hour early each night and go to bed with your Bible instead of your tablet.

Show the enemy you are serious about breaking strongholds and seeing prayers answered in your life and the lives of others.

In the tenth chapter of Daniel, the angel that broke through to meet Daniel told him that his prayers were heard the *very first day* they were prayed! *"Then said he unto me, Fear not, Daniel: for from the first day that thou didst set thine heart to understand, and to chasten thyself before thy God, thy words were heard, and I am come for thy words."* Daniel 10:12 KJV.

Daniel's fast coincided with Passover. It actually preceded it by two weeks. Daniel went above and beyond what was required of him because he wanted to know God, to please Him and to protect and intercede for the Israelites. When he got serious, and started praying and fasting, it shook Heaven and things started happening.

His prayers mattered and they were heard...immediately.

They were not *answered immediately* because he had stirred up a host of trouble. Are we that desperate? Are we that dedicated?

Will we lay aside things other than foods that we love in order to see loved ones saved, relationships restored, prodigals come home, cancers healed, closed wombs opened, and churches full to overflowing?

Please say "YES!" with me today! Let's bind together to see this year be the year of restoration and revival.

It will not happen without sacrifice.

RECIPES

Spaghetti Squash

This recipe is so simple and has gained popularity with those wanting to cut pasta from their diet.

Courtney's Spaghetti Squash

1 Spaghetti Squash
1 large can of tomatoes
2 Tablespoons Garlic
2 Tablespoons Basil
3 Tablespoons Olive Oil
1 teaspoon Salt (or to taste)
1 teaspoon Pepper (or to taste)
1 teaspoon Cayenne pepper (optional)

Cut the Spaghetti Squash in half long ways. Brush with olive oil and then lay flat on a baking sheet. Bake in the oven at 375 degrees for 30-45 minutes. Let cool until you can handle it easily then use a fork to scrape out the squash. It will fall out and look like long strands of spaghetti. You can then season the squash with any spices you choose or just use the sauce to flavor the squash.

Next, in a large pot, brown the olive oil, garlic and basil. In a blender, puree your tomatoes until they are a thick sauce. Pour tomato sauce into pan with olive oil, garlic and basil. Stir in salt and pepper and add 1 teaspoon of cayenne pepper for a little kick if you choose.

7 DESPERATE TIMES, DESPERATE MEASURES

The Bible tells us that the prophet Daniel fasted on a regular basis. It has even recorded three of those fasts for us to look at and observe. In one of them he goes completely without any food at all. *"And I set my face unto the Lord God, to seek by prayer and supplications, with fasting, and sackcloth, and ashes..."* Daniel 9:3 KJV.

In the other two fasts that are recorded in the book of Daniel, he participated in *partial fasts* where he ate some foods, but restrained himself from others.

Each time he fasted, we can find one thing he was very consistent with; he never failed to pray!

Look at the verse above again in Daniel 9:3, *"...to seek by prayer and supplications."* Even when it doesn't specifically mention prayer, we know Daniel prayed because he was a Hebrew prophet and a man of God. He would not have fasted without prayer! The Jewish people understood that the two went together.

Hannah was another child of God who knew what it was like to fast and pray.

Maybe you remember her from the Old Testament book of 1 Samuel. Hannah was married to a wonderful man named Elkanah, who loved her very, very much. But Hannah was not his only wife, as was customary in those days. He had another wife, Peninnah, who was not particularly hospitable. Peninnah had children by Elkanah, but Hannah's womb was barren, and Peninnah loved to boast to (and even torment), poor Hannah about the fact that she was childless!

To not be able to have children in that time period was considered almost a disgrace, and the women took it personally, as if God had cursed them. Remember Sarah who tried to take things in her own hands and insisted Abraham take one of her handmaidens in order to have a child?

Sarah couldn't wait and let God bring about the miracle He had promised!

Every year Elkanah took his family out of the city to sacrifice and worship the Lord in Shiloh. This time was no different. As usual, on the way, Peninnah was being her contrary and annoying self, tormenting poor Hannah to tears.

Hannah would not eat, she was so upset. And we are led to believe she was fasting, for when they arrived at the temple she prayed to the Lord, *"O Lord of hosts, if thou... wilt give unto thine handmaid a man child, then I will give him unto the Lord all the days of his life, and there shall no razor come upon his head."* 1 Samuel 1:11 KJV.

Eli the priest accused her of being drunk because in her deep anguish, her lips moved but no sound came out. She replied, *"No, my lord, I am a woman of a sorrowful spirit: I have drunk neither wine nor strong drink, but have poured out my soul before the Lord."* 1 Samuel 1:15 KJV.

With that, Eli told her to go her way, her prayer had been answered. And true to His Word, God gave Hannah the desire of her heart. True to Hannah's word, she gave her son, Samuel, back to the Lord.

Desperate times? Desperate measures!

Yes, Hannah was so upset she *couldn't* do anything *but* fast! Have you ever been so desperate that you *had to fast*? You had to go to prayer? Your need was so critical that just saying you were praying about it wasn't enough. A bedtime lay-me-down-to-sleep prayer wasn't going to get it. You had to get down to business.

Does that mean we have to work at getting God to answer prayer?

No. We are the ones who need the changing, not God. Fasting changes US, strengthens us, molds our character, changes our heart, mind and soul, gives us direction, wisdom, and clears things up that were *muddy* before!

God can speak to us because we have cleaned things out of our minds. We have taken time to be with Him and pushed some things aside, things that we liked, maybe even loved, that were important to us. We laid them down in order to be with Him.

Praying that we will all become like Hannah, Daniel and many others throughout the centuries who were desperate for God to move in their lives. Fasting WITH prayer not only changes situations but it changes ME!

How desperate are you?

RECIPES

Oven baked fries: Just slice up your potatoes lengthwise and then into steak fries. In a plastic gallon size bag, pour about 1 teaspoon of olive oil and ½ teaspoon paprika, sea salt & pepper. You can add any spices you like and adjust those measurements as needed according to how many potatoes you are using. Then toss in your sliced potatoes and make sure they get coated evenly with the oil and spices. Place on cookie sheet sprayed with cooking spray and bake in oven set on 350 degrees for about 12-15 minutes then turn them over and cook another 10 minutes.

Basic Oil and Vinegar Dressing:
½ cup olive oil, ¼ cup vinegars (mixed) or lemon juice, ½ cup water, 1 Tablespoon garlic powder, salt and pepper. (Remember, Paul Newman's Oil and Vinegar Dressing is Daniel Fast approved).

Salad: Lettuce, red onion, unsweetened dried fruit, (may also add sliced oranges, apples, grapes, etc.) toasted nuts and dressing.

Four Bean Salads: 1 can each of kidney beans, yellow waxed beans, green beans and butter beans, drained. 1 T. garlic powder, ½ sliced red onion, 1 sliced red pepper, oil and vinegar dressing.

Baked Sweet Potatoes topped with chopped pineapple and nutmeg!

Oatmeal cooked with chopped apples and raisins, topped with chopped raw almonds!

If you like cold cereal, you can have Kashi Puffs and unsweetened soy or almond milk, topped with fresh strawberries and bananas or peaches and blueberries. Eat only the Kashi 7 Whole Grain Puffs! The others have added cane sugar.

You are catching on! Go with God...

8 BIND THE STRONG MAN!

We have discussed in earlier posts that Jesus told His disciples that some things do not get taken care of except by prayer *and* fasting. Matthew 17:14-21.

If you are fasting for others, a loved one, a prodigal, someone dear to you for whatever reason...these battles of spiritual warfare will take dominion over the power of the enemy!

Ephesians 6:12 KJV. *"For we wrestle not against flesh and blood, but against principalities, against powers, against the rulers of the darkness of this world, against spiritual wickedness in high places."*

Our fight is not with flesh and blood, or with people, but it is against the *powers that influence people.*

This is a spiritual battle, seen or unseen. We must have a disciplined prayer life and couple that with regular fasting!

Fasting breaks strongholds! It can literally set people free from the chains that bind them. But in order to do that, that strong man must be taken care of first.

Did you catch that verse? The strong man is Satan and he has *slaves* that do his bidding and are yoked, or bound, to wickedness.

But prayer WITH fasting can literally break that yoke and set people free from bondage!

Then they will be able to come to God without hindrance.

Remember, we saw in Daniel 10 when he was fasting for 21 days that angels were loosed to fight on his behalf. They literally had to fight devils in order to get a word from God to Daniel. His prayer and fasting were shaking things up.

Prayers were answered; chains were broken.

So what are you fasting, praying and believing God to do for you? Get that Bible out and start reading scripture out loud when you pray. Take authority in the Spirit and watch what happens while you are on this fast. You may face opposition...but keep pressing in and pressing on. The battle is the Lord's; you are just clay in the Potter's hands. He will take care of His own!

RECIPES

Apple slices - dipped in raw almond butter mixed with a drizzle of honey (if you are using honey). It is also good without!

Tortilla Soup

½ cup celery, chopped
1 medium onion, diced fine
1 medium zucchini, chopped
1 medium yellow squash, chopped
2 cups frozen corn
2 tomatoes, chopped
2 garlic cloves, minced
8 cups vegetable broth
4 cups water
1 can of black or kidney beans
¼ cup chopped cilantro
Sea salt
Juice of one lime

6-8 corn tortillas
Olive Oil

Heat enough oil to sauté the first four ingredients. Add everything else except the tortillas. Simmer for at least 30 minutes or can add to crockpot and cook on low four hours. Brush tortillas with olive oil and cut into strips. Bake in oven for about 15 minutes on 350 degrees. Top with tortilla strips, green onion and even avocado to serve.

Apple Pecan Salad

2 apples, peeled and diced
¼ cup pecans, halved
1 handful of bagged salad mixture
Juice of 1 orange
1 Tablespoon olive oil

Place salad in bottom of bowl. Add apple chunks, then celery. Top with pecans. Place orange juice and olive oil in a small jar with a tight fitting lid and shake to mix well. Pour over salad as dressing.

Blessings to you as you continue on your fast. God is well pleased when we deny ourselves things that we enjoy and concentrate more on Him.

9 REBUILDING THE WALLS

We all know we *need* to fast; some of us just need to be encouraged to do so! Jesus didn't say, *"If we fast"*. He said *"When ye fast..."* Matthew 6:16-18.

The prophet Nehemiah fasted when he heard that his beloved city of Jerusalem had been reduced to ruins.

Nehemiah was heartbroken at the news he had received of his homeland.

He sat down.

He cried.

He mourned.

For days.

He fasted.

He prayed.

He asked for mercy when he went before the king. He also humbly asked for permission, for caution and wisdom. Then he headed to Jerusalem to rebuild the walls!

Have the walls of your life been broken down?

Does the enemy of your soul lie to you and torment you on every turn?

Are you filled with anxiety, fear and dread every day?

Weep, mourn, fast, pray, ask for caution and wisdom. Then what?

Start rebuilding the walls!

Put your faith and confidence in the One who delivers, heals, restores and brings peace to a troubled mind. Let Him give you the strength to put one stone upon another and rebuild the walls in your life.

Nehemiah was sold out and committed. The wall is being rebuilt and he is in charge. The people are under fear of attack at any time. So they work from sunrise to sunset with half of the men always on guard. They never even took off their clothes, and carried their weapons with them at all times, even when they went for water. *"...The laborers carried on their work with one hand supporting their load and one hand holding a weapon."* Nehemiah 4:17

Nehemiah, and those working with him, would not come down off of the wall until the job was completed! They didn't sit down and whine and complain that it was too hard. They didn't stop the work and wait for the attack that they knew was inevitable. They kept on working and yet were vigilant at the same time. What faith!

Nehemiah even tells them in verse 19, *"...the work is very spread out, and we are widely separated from each other along the wall. When you hear the blast of the trumpet, rush to wherever it is sounding. Then our God will fight for us!"*

Nehemiah knew he couldn't do it alone. It took fasting, prayer and being totally committed to the work and cause of the Kingdom. He never gave up.

God answers prayers of sacrifice, desperation and commitment. What are you praying for today?

RECIPES

Veggies in a Flat Wrap

2 WHOLE GRAIN flatbread wraps
1 cup shredded carrot
1 cup shredded zucchini
¼ cup red onion, diced fine (optional)
1 Tablespoon apple cider vinegar
Sea salt and pepper to taste
4 Tablespoons hummus

Combine carrot, zucchini, onion, apple cider vinegar, salt, and pepper in a bowl and toss well to make a slaw. Spread your hummus over the tortilla wraps. Place a handful of slaw on top of the hummus. Grind some fresh pepper over top and add a few pumpkin seeds or other favorite seeds. Roll up the wraps and serve!

All Wrapped Up Salad

2 WHOLE GRAIN wraps
½ ripe avocado
1 carrot, shredded
1 cucumber, diced
¼ teaspoon of oregano (or your favorite seasoning)
1 ripe tomato, diced
Handful of fresh spinach, chopped fine
½ sweet red onion, diced
1 teaspoon extra virgin olive oil (or favorite dressing)
Dash of Salt
Dash of cayenne to taste

Prepare all veggies. Mash avocado and spread in the center of the wrap. Add remaining ingredients and roll up, tucking in ends as you roll. You can vary the amounts of each vegetable or add or subtract different veggies according to individual tastes.

Also, you are missing out if you haven't fixed a big old-fashioned *fruit salad*! When was the last time you bought a fresh pineapple? Slice that baby into bite-sized pieces, add blueberries, strawberries, green or red grapes, orange sections (or even mandarin oranges in a can are great in a fruit salad!) diced apples, bananas (the pineapple will take care of any browning of the bananas), and any other fruit that you favor. Put it in pretty parfait glasses, or a big glass serving bowl and it will be the shining star of your breakfast, lunch or dinner table!

Remember, three small meals a day and two small snacks, (optional), should be more than enough on the Daniel Fast. Be sure you are drinking plenty of water. It is unlimited! You need to stay hydrated.

Be blessed!

10 TO OPEN THEIR EYES

We have discovered in the last few days that prayer and fasting together have the power to tear down strongholds, to shake heaven and give us strength to overcome.

Saul was the biggest persecutor of the early Church. He didn't just talk about his hatred of Christians, he literally had them hauled out of their homes and into the streets, beaten and then sent to prison! He showed no mercy. On the road to Damascus, he and those traveling with him were struck by a blinding light. The Lord asked him why he was persecuting Him and instructed Paul to go into the city where he would be told what to do.

It is not clear whether Saul (who was later called Paul) ***chose*** this particular fast or not. We will assume that he did! After an encounter like he had just experienced, who would feel like eating? He waits the three days. He cannot see. He isn't eating, and he isn't drinking.

I'll bet Saul is doing a whole lot of thinking.

"What is going on? What is going to happen to ME? I have been persecuting these people that are chosen of God for years and now I find out who HE really is. The Messiah! What is HE going to do with ME? Go into the city and wait? Wait, for what?"

Jesus *did* have plans for Saul. Without Saul, (here Jesus changes his name to Paul), we wouldn't have 13 of the 27 books of the New Testament. Jesus had intentions for him to be the rocket that helped launch the Gospel around the world. As he stands before King Agrippa, Paul explains to him in detail what happened on that road so long ago.

"But rise, and stand upon thy feet: for I have appeared unto thee for this purpose, to make thee a minister and a witness both of these things which thou hast seen, and of those things in the which I will appear unto thee; Delivering thee from the people and from the Gentiles, unto whom I send thee, To open their eyes, and to turn them from darkness to light, and from the power of Satan unto God, that they may receive forgiveness of sins, and inheritance among them which are sanctified by faith that is in me." Acts 26:16-18 KJV.

To open their eyes just as Paul's eyes were opened.

We have the ability through prayer and fasting, to help open the eyes of those that are lost, those that are blinded by the darkness of this world, and help them to see the Light and the Truth that is in Jesus Christ.

God wants to deliver them from this darkness and bring them into His Kingdom.

That is where we come in. We must have a burden for souls, which only comes out of consistent prayer and fasting.

"If my people, which are called by my name, shall humble themselves, and pray, and seek my face, and turn from their wicked ways; then will I hear from heaven, and will forgive their sin, and will heal their land." 2 Chronicles 7:14 KJV.

Humbling ourselves, denying ourselves, realizing without Him we are nothing but *with* Him we are powerful and unstoppable…then He will heal our land! Prayer and fasting can set our friends, neighbors, and family free from the chains that have them bound so they can be like Paul: their eyes can be opened to see Truth and see who Jesus really is.

THAT is powerful!

Recipes and Variations!

Oatmeal

1 cup oatmeal *(not instant)* with ¼ cup chopped apples, 2 Tablespoons raisins, 1 Tablespoon chopped walnuts and a pinch of cinnamon.

Peanut Butter Banana Smoothie

Here is a great morning pick-me-up/on-the-go recipe. We have mentioned that on the Daniel Fast you drink only water, and yet I am posting a second smoothie recipe. Most usually the smoothies are used as ***meal replacements*** on the Daniel Fast, not as a treat, dessert or a reward.

Smoothies are filling and really do not need anything else to go with them. *Remember you ARE fasting.*

This one calls for peanut butter, but it is NOT regular peanut butter. This is natural peanut butter without added sugar, which is easy to find in the same location as the others, just read the label. There are good organic peanut butters and there are store brand peanut butters with no added sugar.

All you need is a banana, *(I freeze mine! Peel and wrap them in plastic wrap. When you need one just let it sit out about ten minutes. This replaces the ice.)*
2-3 Tablespoons of natural peanut butter
A splash or two of unsweetened almond milk
Blend together and you have breakfast!

Flatbread with Salad

3 cups fresh baby spinach topped with sliced strawberries, orange sections, sliced almonds, 1½ teaspoon olive oil and apple cider vinegar, 1 whole-wheat, WHOLE GRAIN, flatbread. Layer in order and devour!

Easy Veggie Flatbread

1 sliced tomato
1 small sliced bell pepper
¼ cup chopped jalapenos
½ cup hummus
1½ oz. whole-wheat flatbread

Spread hummus on flatbread, assemble toppings!

11 NOT BY BREAD ALONE

How did Jesus fight temptation from the enemy when He was fasting? With the Word of God!

If you have been struggling while on the Daniel Fast, finding it hard to do without the things that you enjoy the most, maybe it is time to get out your sword. Let's fight some temptation today!

"It is written, Man shall not live by bread alone, but by every word that proceedeth out of the mouth of God." Matthew 4:4 KJV.

"No temptation has seized you except what is common to man. And God is faithful; he will not let you be tempted beyond what you can bear. But when you are tempted, he will also provide a way out so that you can stand up under it." 1 Corinthians 10:13 NIV.

"Consider it pure joy, my brothers, whenever you face trials of many kinds, because you know that the testing of your faith develops perseverance. Perseverance must finish its work so that you may be mature and complete, not lacking anything." James 1:2-4 NIV.

"Submit yourselves, then, to God. Resist the devil, and he will flee from you." James 4:7 NIV.

"And lead us not into temptation, but deliver us from evil." Matthew 6:13 KJV.

"Watch and pray that you may not enter into temptation. The spirit indeed is willing, but the flesh is weak." Matthew 26:41 NKJV.

"Be sober, be vigilant; because your adversary the devil, as a roaring lion, walketh about, seeking whom he may devour: Whom resist stedfast in the faith, knowing that the same afflictions are accomplished in your brethren that are in the world." 1 Peter 5:8-9 KJV.

There is power and authority in the Word of God; use it to overcome the temptations of the enemy, whether they are physical or spiritual.

Take these scriptures and make them your own. With this shorter lesson today you have time to find some others in the Word and pray them out loud, building up your most holy faith.

RECIPES

Crazy Slow Cooker Soup

1¾ cups fresh green beans
1½ cups sliced onions
2 large yellow or zucchini squash, cut in 1 inch chunks
2 bell peppers cut in narrow strips or diced
2 large potatoes cut in ½ inch chunks
1 clove garlic, minced
Large can stewed tomatoes
6 oz. can tomato sauce
2 Tablespoons olive oil
½ teaspoon sea salt or to taste (optional). Mix ingredients in a crock pot. Cook on high four hours or all day on low. Enjoy!

12 WHEN OTHERS INTERCEDE

Are you falling in love with the book of Daniel? This prophet is quite a guy. Just look at what others thought about him. *"Then this Daniel was preferred above the presidents and princes, because an excellent spirit was in him..."* Daniel 6:3 KJV.

An excellent spirit was in him. He was loved, he was trusted, and he was *preferred.* Other translations say *"...he proved himself more capable."*

The other administrators and officers were a little bit jealous and tried to find fault with him. They could find none. They decided they would try to trip him up concerning *"...his God."*

They came up with a plan, and approached King Darius, asking him to make a declaration that if anyone prayed to someone, or something, other than the king for the next 30 days they would be thrown into the den of lions.

When Daniel heard of the decree, he did what he did EVERY day: at the time of prayer he opened his window toward Jerusalem and he prayed, three times a day, just as he had always done before the decree.

Immediately the *prayer police* went running to King Darius and reminded him of the decree and informed him that one certain Daniel-the-Prophet was breaking the rules.

The king was extremely upset because he was so fond of Daniel, yet he had no choice but to follow through with the consequences because *rules are rules* and he was the king!

As soon as they put Daniel into the den of lions, the king's faith went into action, *"Thy God whom thou servest continually, he will deliver thee."*

What a great example of faith from a man who doesn't even know the God of Daniel? He believes in Daniel and so he believes in his God.

They sealed the den with a stone, the king put *his seal* on it and he headed back to his palace.

So what did he do? He went to his palace and fasted all night long. He didn't eat, he didn't sleep and he did not listen to music!

See the variation of fasts? No food, no sleep and no social media!

Sorry, wrong century. No music, in the king's situation.

The next morning he ran to the den and called for Daniel, *"Daniel, O Daniel, servant of the living God, is thy God, whom thou servest continually, able to deliver thee from the lions?"*

"My God hath sent his angel, and hath shut the lions' mouths, that they have not hurt me: forasmuch as before him innocency was found in me; and also before thee, O king, have I done no hurt." Daniel 6:20-22 KJV.

Delivered.

Saved.

Rescued by Almighty God.

Intercession was made for Daniel by a friend. Fasting and an all-night prayer meeting by the king and David's life was spared.

Is there power in fasting and prayer?

Day after day we are finding more and more wonderful stories in the Bible, true stories of encouragement and real testimonies of how *God used ordinary people to change history*. Who do you need to intercede for today; to make a difference?

Praying for you that our God will continue to strengthen you, give you peace and answer your prayers according to His will for your life.

RECIPES

Oven Roasted Potatoes

1 cup olive oil
3 pounds potatoes, quartered
2 lemons, juiced
1 clove fresh garlic, minced
¼ cup finely chopped yellow onion
1 Tablespoon dried oregano
1 teaspoon paprika
¼ cup fresh parsley, roughly chopped
Salt and Pepper

Preheat oven to 425 degrees. To make dressing: place olive oil, lemon juice, garlic, onion, oregano and parsley in a food processor. Add 1 teaspoon salt; puree until smooth. Adjust seasoning with black pepper and more salt if needed. Toss the potatoes in a large bowl with ½ cup of the dressing. Spread in a single layer on a large cookie sheet (you may want to line with foil or parchment paper). Place in preheated oven turning occasionally for 45-60 minutes until the potatoes are tender and golden brown. Serve the potatoes drizzled with more dressing.

13 CHOSEN, COMMITTED & COMMISSIONED

Prayer and fasting is not just for emergencies. It isn't only to see fire rain down from heaven, or for God to deliver men from a den of lions. Sometimes, as we are going to see in the Book of Acts, men fasted and prayed, asking God's blessing on something they were about to do.

We still practice that today, and we should always seek the Lord for His direction in the big, and the small, things in our life.

Barnabas wanted to take Saul (Paul) to Antioch. This elder in the Church saw something in the new convert that the others were not aware of quite yet. Barnabas was Paul's teacher, his mentor, and he knew God had big plans in store for this former persecutor of the Church.

"As they ministered to the Lord, and fasted, the Holy Ghost said, 'Separate me Barnabas and Saul for the work whereunto I have called them.' And when they had fasted and prayed, and laid their hands on them, they sent them away." Acts 13:2-3 KJV.

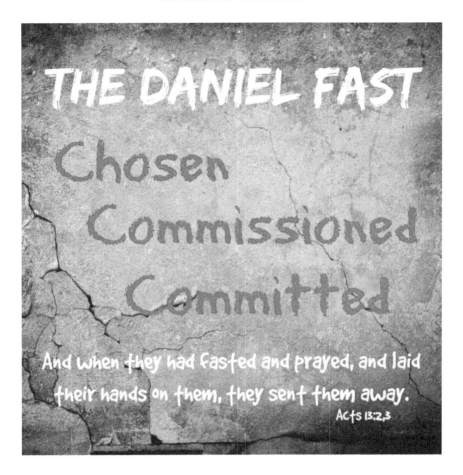

Chosen, commissioned and committed. Barnabas and Paul were sent out as the very first missionaries. They did exactly what Jesus had commanded before He ascended, *"…Go ye into all the world, and preach the gospel to every creature."* Mark 16:15 KJV.

Are you committed? Are you sold out to the cause of Christ? If you have been on the Daniel Fast for any amount of time at all you must be committed to something. You have a desire to live for God, and have a longing to draw closer to Him in the New Year. You surely have a yearning to see your loved ones saved, financial needs met, and to get things in your life turned around to where Jesus is finally *first*.

You are on the right track! Regular prayer and fasting, daily prayer and digging in the Word of God will see you moving in the right direction.

If you want a personal relationship with Jesus Christ, you must spend time with Him. If you never communicate, you cannot know Him. If you never talk to your husband or wife, there is rarely any communication, that relationship is not going to last very long. If it is a new relationship, it will not even get off of the ground.

Take time to get to know the Savior. He is waiting for you.

Fasting moves things out of your heart that shouldn't be there and illuminates things that you didn't realize had moved in.

"Separate me Barnabas and Saul for the work whereunto I have called them...." is what the Holy Ghost said.

Strive to be separated, through regular prayer and fasting, and see what God will do through you.

RECIPES

Stuffed Peppers

3 cups cooked brown rice, divided
1 cup frozen corn thawed
2 green onions, chopped
¼ cup chopped fresh cilantro
2 Tablespoons olive oil
2 Tablespoons fresh lime juice
1 clove garlic minced
Salt & Pepper to taste
2-3 large bell peppers cut in half lengthwise and cored
2 cups 100% vegetable or tomato juice

Preheat oven to 350 degrees. Using a large bowl, gently combine 1 cup of brown rice, corn, green onions, cilantro, oil, lime juice and garlic. Place the pepper halves in a large glass baking dish and stuff them with the rice mixture. Spoon some of the juice over the peppers and pour the remainder of the juice into the dish. Cover and bake for 45-60 minutes.

To serve, place about ½ cup of the reserved rice on each plate, add a pepper and a little juice over the top. *Makes four servings.*

Blessings to you on your journey while denying your flesh and drawing closer to God. You will see revival in your church, your family and your world!

14 JONAH: AND GOD SAW

Poor Jonah.

God told him to go to Nineveh to preach to the wicked people to change their ways or He would destroy them.

Jonah refused. He made a beeline for Tarshish, via Joppa, and hopped a boat, where he made all kinds of trouble.

The men on the boat discovered he must be the cause of the mayhem, since the ship was about to sink. Jonah confessed that he was the one they were looking for, and even though they did not wish to do so, they threw him overboard.

Picked up by a giant fish, he spent three nights in the belly of this overgrown sea lion, not the most pleasant of accommodations. *"Then Jonah prayed unto the Lord his God out of the fish's belly..."* Jonah 2:1 KJV.

Confession is good for the soul, especially in Jonah's case. *"And the Lord spake unto the fish, and it vomited out Jonah upon the dry land."* Jonah 2:10 KJV.

Now what? Surely saying he was sorry was good enough and he could go back home.

Not so fast Jonah. *"And the word of the Lord came unto Jonah the second time, saying, Arise, go unto Nineveh, that great city, and preach unto it the preaching that I bid thee."* Jonah 3:1, 2 KJV.

The second time. This time Jonah was in no position to argue; he wasn't about to. He didn't even want to imagine where he might end up next.

He headed straight for the city of Nineveh. When he arrived, he immediately did what the Lord commanded.

He preached. He told them they needed to repent because in 40 days the city would be overthrown.

The people believed God!

"So the people of Nineveh believed God, and proclaimed a fast, and put on sackcloth, from the greatest of them even to the least of them." Jonah 3:5 KJV.

Sackcloth was a sign of repentance and humility.

Word had come from the king himself, he had taken off his robe, covered himself in sackcloth and sat in ashes! He said,

"Let neither man nor beast, herd nor flock, taste any thing: let them not feed, nor drink water: But let man and beast be covered with sackcloth, and cry mightily unto God: yea, let them turn every one from his evil way, and from the violence that is in their hands. Who can tell if God will turn and repent, and turn away from his fierce anger, that we perish not?" Jonah 3:7-9 KJV.

The entire city believed the Word of the Lord and they repented. Everyone, even all of their animals, went on a fast. They did not even drink water for what appears to be three days.

The desperate situation called for desperate measures as we have talked about earlier in our studies. They humbled their souls with fasting and what happened?

"And God saw their works, that they turned from their evil way; and God repented of the evil, that he had said that he would do unto them; and he did it not." Jonah 3:3-10 KJV.

Did they change the mind of God? Of course they did!

Repentance, a broken spirit, turning from sin and turning *to* God for forgiveness will cause the Lord to reach out a hand of *MERCY*.

This is what Jehovah wanted them to do.

It was not His desire to destroy the city, or else He would not have sent Jonah there to warn them. It was His desire that they repent and turn from their wicked way.

Thankfully, this king had a repentant heart and turned his people back to God.

He humbled his soul with fasting and his people followed him. He saved an entire city from destruction by the humility of prayer and fasting!

"And God saw…And God repented…And He did it not."

Are you struggling with something that needs forgiveness? Is there something or someone that you cannot forgive? Is it really worth it to hold a grudge? Do you realize it is only hurting YOU? Let it go. Tomorrow may be too late. Pray, fast, break the chains that are holding you back and start living the life God intends for you to live.

Today.

RECIPES

Here is a great tip for *almost-over-ripe bananas*. Peel them, cut them up and freeze them. *(We have already mentioned freezing bananas for smoothies, they are great!)* You can take them out and thaw them for your oatmeal, adding a great sweetness, no need for sugar.

Then, those same frozen bananas, thrown into the food processor with 1-2 Tablespoons of water for about five minutes, will make a delicious soft serve ***ice cream***. You *are* allowed two snacks on the Daniel Fast; just don't overdo it. It *is* just a banana.

Hot & Fruity Brown Rice Cereal
1 cup almond milk
2 cups cooked brown rice
1 apple, chopped, unpeeled (about 1½ cups)
1 banana, mashed (about 1 cup)
1 cup chopped dates or raisins
1½ teaspoons cinnamon
Pinch of nutmeg and ¼ cup toasted pecans or walnuts

Add milk, brown rice, apple, banana, dates, cinnamon, and nutmeg to a medium saucepan. Cook over medium-low heat about 10 minutes, or until heated through. Stir frequently to prevent burning. Sprinkle one Tablespoon pecans or walnuts over each serving.

15 CORNELIUS, THERE IS MORE!

Every time I read the amazing story of Cornelius I get goose bumps. Don't you? Are you familiar with this devout man? Let me tell you what God says about him…

"There was a certain man in Caesarea called Cornelius, a centurion of the band called the Italian band, A devout man, and one that feared God with all his house, which gave much alms to the people, and prayed to God alway." Acts 10:1, 2 KJV.

A centurion was a captain over 100 soldiers; he was a fairly important man. The Bible says he was *devout*, he feared God, meaning he revered Him, and made sure those in his household did the same. He also gave of his tithes and offerings and prayed to the Lord always.

In our language, He was a Bible-believing, church-going, tithe-paying, God-fearing, all-around good guy! It was obvious he loved God and prayed to Him every day.

So then, why did the Lord insist that Peter go and visit Cornelius?

There are a couple of reasons. One of them Peter wasn't so crazy about at first.

The Jews and the Gentiles didn't mix, for lack of a better way to put it. The Gospel had not yet been preached to the rest of the world. The Jews had pretty much determined it belonged to them exclusively.

When Peter fell into a trance on the rooftop he saw all of these *unclean* animals that the Israelites are not supposed to eat and the Lord tells him, *"Rise Peter, kill and eat!"*

Peter immediately says, "No way, Lord! I have never eaten anything common or unclean!" (I'm taking liberty to paraphrase just a little here). This happens three times and then the vessel with the unclean animals is taken away and Peter wakes up.

Immediately, there is a knock at his door. The Lord speaks to Peter and tells him that he is to go with these men and that He has sent them, not to worry, not to doubt. What a promise!

Cornelius had also heard from God to send for Peter and when Peter arrives he tells him what has happened,

"And Cornelius said, Four days ago I was fasting until this hour; and at the ninth hour I prayed in my house, and, behold, a man stood before me in bright clothing…" Acts 10:30 KJV.

So Peter realizes that this is *BIG*. And he preaches the first sermon to the Gentile people by saying these famous words:

"Of a truth I perceive that God is no respecter of persons…"

"That word, I say, ye know, which was published throughout all Judaea, and began from Galilee, after the baptism which John preached; How God anointed Jesus of Nazareth with the Holy Ghost and with power: who went about doing good, and healing all that were oppressed of the devil; for God was with him…"

He preaches for a couple of moments and ends up with *"...that through his name whosoever believeth in him shall receive remission of sins."* Acts 10:37-43 KJV.

Now, here come the goose bumps!

"While Peter yet spake these words, the Holy Ghost fell on all them which heard the word. And they of the circumcision which believed were astonished, as many as came with Peter, because that on the Gentiles also was poured out the gift of the Holy Ghost. For they heard them speak with tongues, and magnify God." Acts 10:44-46 KJV.

What? You mean *this is why* Peter was sent to Cornelius?

Did he not already KNOW God?

Did he not pray every day?

Was he not a good man?

Didn't he pay his tithe?

Didn't He fear God and give Him reverence?

Didn't he give to the poor?

Why then did he need Peter to come?

What else did he need to know?

Cornelius needed MORE….

Cornelius didn't have the Holy Ghost!

Cornelius had only been baptized with the baptism of John!

While Peter was PREACHING, the Holy Ghost literally *FELL* on those that were listening, just like it did in the second chapter of Acts.

How do we know something actually happened? Because the WORD says so! *"For they HEARD them SPEAK with TONGUES and MAGNIFY GOD."* Acts 10:46 KJV.

God sent Peter to tell Cornelius that what he had was not enough.

John's baptism was not enough. He needed to be re-baptized in the Name of Jesus *and* he needed the infilling of the Holy Spirit!

Well, you may say, that was then and this is now. If the Bible says it isn't so, then it isn't so. But if the Bible says it is for us today...

Peter cleared up that confusion in Acts 2:39 when he said, *"For the promise is unto you, and to your children, and to all that are afar off, even as many as the Lord our God shall call."*

The Holy Ghost wasn't an extra added blessing for just a few.

Over and over in the Book of Acts (the birthing of the Church) they repeat the example:

"And when the day of Pentecost was fully come, they were all with one accord in one place. And suddenly there came a sound from heaven as of a rushing mighty wind, and it filled all the house where they were sitting. And there appeared unto them cloven tongues like as of fire, and it sat upon each of them, And they were all filled with the Holy Ghost, and began to speak with other tongues, as the Spirit gave them utterance." Acts 2:1-4 KJV.

"Then Peter said unto them, Repent, and be baptized every one of you in the name of Jesus Christ for the remission of sins, and ye shall receive the gift of the Holy Ghost." Acts 2:38 KJV.

"Now when the apostles which were at Jerusalem heard that Samaria had received the word of God, they sent unto them Peter and John: Who, when they were come down, prayed for them, that they might receive the Holy Ghost: (For as yet he was fallen upon none of them: only they were baptized in the name of the Lord Jesus.) Then laid they their hands on them, and they received the Holy Ghost." Acts 8:14-17 KJV.

"And it came to pass, that, while Apollos was at Corinth, Paul having passed through the upper coasts came to Ephesus: and finding certain disciples, He said unto them, Have ye received the Holy Ghost since ye believed? And they said unto him, We have not so much as heard whether there be any Holy Ghost. And he said unto them, Unto what then were ye baptized? And they said, Unto John's baptism. Then said Paul, John verily baptized with the baptism of repentance, saying unto the people, that they should believe on him which should come after him, that is, on Christ Jesus. When they heard this, they were baptized in the name of the Lord Jesus. And when Paul had laid his hands upon them, the Holy Ghost came on them; and they spake with tongues, and prophesied." Acts 19:1-6 KJV.

Such wonderful words; such confirmation! Look at Ephesus again. Paul asks them, *"Have you received **the power** (Holy Ghost) since you believed?"* Remember, the Lord said you would receive *power* after that the Holy Ghost has come upon you! (Acts 1)

The people at Ephesus hadn't even heard of the Holy Ghost. So Paul, just like Peter, asked how they were baptized. They replied, *"John's baptism."* But John's baptism was only a *baptism of repentance* and he pointed them to the One that should come after. Once again, what did they do?

They were baptized in the NAME of the LORD JESUS!

Then what happened?

They spoke with tongues and prophesied! They spoke with tongues and magnified God!

Remember, Jesus told them to *"...wait for the promise of the Father..."* and that He would *"send the Comforter..."* He did that in the Upper Room. (Acts 2) They were waiting just like He said and the Holy Ghost came as a mighty rushing wind. It has never stopped in over 2,000 years!

Why would something as magnificent as the Holy Ghost, so life-changing, only be for a few?

If He filled all of those people in the Book of Acts, why would it stop? Why would He say, "Now, as soon as all of the apostles have been martyred, the outpouring of the Holy Ghost will cease." He did not.

Brothers, sisters, we are Acts CHAPTER 29! *"For the promise is unto you, and to your children, and to all that are afar off, even as many as the Lord our God shall call."* Acts 2:39 KJV.

Stand on the Word today, just because *man* has changed it, *man* has doctored it, *man* has watered it down, doesn't mean it isn't there in black and white.

It doesn't mean it isn't for you.

Cornelius fasted, he believed, he received; he *and* his household.

And the Holy Ghost fell!

In these last days we need that infilling of His spirit now more than ever.

RECIPES

Corn Muffins

1 ½ cup yellow cornmeal
¾ cup unsweetened almond milk
¼ cup water
1 Tablespoon Date Butter
1 Tablespoon olive oil
¾ cup frozen corn kernels
¼ cup chopped green onions
½ teaspoon salt

Preheat oven to 400 degrees. Mix cornmeal, almond milk, water, date butter and olive oil in a medium bowl. Stir. Add corn, green onions, and salt. Stir until well combined. Lightly rub a mini-muffin tin with olive oil. Fill all 24 cups about ¾ full. Bake 15 minutes. If using a regular muffin tin, fill all 12 cups about ¾ full and bake 20 minutes. The muffins go well with so many of the soups on the Daniel Fast!

Date Butter

1½ cup dates
1¼ cup water
¾ teaspoon cinnamon
¼ teaspoon nutmeg
½ teaspoon vanilla

Bring dates and water to boil in small pan, making sure the dates are covered in the water. Reduce heat to low and simmer about 45-60 minutes. Dates will break down and soften. Cool for about 15 minutes. Puree entire mixture in blender until smooth then add cinnamon and nutmeg, mix well. *Date butter can be used quite often during the fast for several recipes so you can make it ahead and keep it in the refrigerator until needed.*

Quick Broccoli Salad

1 head fresh broccoli, chopped into small pieces
1 small red onion, diced
1 cup sliced fresh mushrooms
1 cup cherry tomatoes, sliced in half
Paul Newman's Own Oil & Vinegar dressing

Mix all ingredients together, pouring dressing over salad. Let this sit 2-4 hours in the refrigerator before serving.

16 EXCEPT YE ABIDE

Revival is not coming friends...it is HERE!

The Book of Acts only has 28 chapters and we are looking at number 27 today. Paul was running out of time. He was being taken to Rome to stand trial, (along with some other political prisoners), and ultimately, eventually, he would become a martyr for the cause of Christ.

But the issue at hand was the ship.

He was in the hands of a capable man. Julius was a centurion who was the commander of a *cohort*. A cohort is a band of soldiers between 400-600 men. This was a large ship and quite full! The end of the chapter tells us there were a total of 276 people on board.

They had already changed boats and changed routes, because of the weather. Choosing the longer course meant they could use the island of Cypress to shield them from the rough seas, or so they hoped.

The inhabitants of the ship had stopped in the city of Fair Havens for a time. It doesn't say how long, but Paul and others aboard had been fasting, since it was the time of The Day of Atonement, or Yom Kippur. They realized they were facing rough weather ahead and Paul tried to convince them to stay in Fair Havens and wait it out.

"Now when much time was spent, and when sailing was now dangerous, because the fast was now already past, Paul admonished them, And said unto them, Sirs, I perceive that this voyage will be with hurt and much damage, not only of the lading and ship, but also of our lives. Nevertheless the centurion believed the master and the owner of the ship, more than those things which were spoken by Paul." Acts 27:9-11 KJV.

Here is the dilemma: God had revealed to Paul that the weather was to become perilous and for them to *stay* where they were. Paul warned Julius, but do not forget that Paul is also a PRISONER. Julius was in quite a predicament. He had the experience of the pilot and captain in one ear, and this *man of God* in the other.

What they wanted to do doesn't sound so bad. It would have only taken them a day to get to Phoenix and that didn't seem like such a risk. It was a bigger town. It was close to Fair Havens and better protected from the weather. The sailors would be thrilled because there was more to do there.

But God said, *"Stay. Abide."*

"But Lord, I see a storm coming!"

Does this sound like anyone else you know? Or does it sound like ME or YOU?

How many times do we go ahead and do what *we* want to do even though God says, *"STAY."*

He wants us to wait, listen, and trust Him. But we insist on doing our own thing anyway.

So the ship sets sail.

"But not long after there arose against it a tempestuous wind, called Euroclydon." Acts 27:14 KJV.

This wind was so strong that it had a name. Things started happening quickly. The second day they begin to lighten the ship, throwing things overboard.

"On the third day, they threw the ships tackle overboard with their own hands." Acts 27:19 NIV.

Now, they were getting rid of some of the ship's gear. Desperation had set in. If only they had listened to Paul!

"When neither sun nor stars appeared for many days and the storm continued raging, we finally gave up all hope of being saved." Acts 10:20 NIV.

They were in trouble; big trouble. They should have listened. They should have stayed in Fair Havens to begin with but they didn't. All hope was gone as far as they were concerned.

How many times have we all been in the same situation as the crew of this ship? How many of us, just like Julius, have rejected the voice of God and did things our own way, only to fail miserably?

Did God make us come crawling on our hands and knees begging Him to take us back? Never, and He doesn't require it of these men either.

He shows mercy.

Paul stands before them and brings them good news. *"And now I exhort you to be of good cheer: for there shall be no loss of any man's life among you, but of the ship. For there stood by me this night the angel of God, whose I am, and whom I serve, Saying, Fear not, Paul; thou must be brought before Caesar: and, lo, God hath given thee all them that sail with thee…**for I believe God, that it shall be even as it was told me.**"* Acts 10:22-25 KJV.

Even after he gave them this great news, the storm grew worse and some of the men tried to abandon the ship. We may have done the same in a state of panic!

But Paul tells Julius and the soldiers, *"Except these abide in the ship, ye cannot be saved."*

The next morning, Paul urged them to eat because it had been 14 days since they had begun fasting. They needed their strength.

He reminds them that God had promised that not a hair on their head would be harmed as long as they stayed in the ship!

After they had eaten, those 276 souls lightened the ship even more by throwing over the wheat. Do you see a pattern here?

Stay in the ship!

Abide with Him!

Get rid of those things that would keep you from walking with God, that would pull you down or drag you under. A little hindrance, a stumbling block...nothing is worth losing your soul.

The ship began to break apart in the back and the prisoners and crew grabbed hold of pieces of debris and broken planks to swim to shore. Not one of them perished!

"And so it came to pass, that they escaped all safe to land." Acts 27:44 KJV.

Paul had been fasting, he was a man of prayer, and he had been shipwrecked two times previously. He trusted God when he heard His voice. He was strengthened by his time of prayer and fasting. God gave him wisdom to handle this situation and hold everything together.

Why else would a commander of an army trust a prisoner to give direction?

Only God would allow that to take place.

When we allow Him to have the authority in our lives, to rule, to give the direction and wisdom for every aspect and every detail, knowing He sees down the road...we don't have to worry about the end result. He has it all in control!

Did you know He also *cares*? He wants what is best for us. The ultimate goal is our salvation and eternity in heaven with Him.

Believe that today. There is safety in the ship. Trust Him in the storms. If you decide you want to go running off in another direction, He cannot promise your safety.

Except ye abide...

RECIPES

Black Bean & Pineapple Salad

1 can pineapple chunks, drained
1 can black beans, rinsed and drained
1 ½ cups brown rice
½ cup chopped bell pepper
¼ cup chopped celery

If you are using honey during your fast, you can make an easy honey mustard dressing with ¼ cup yellow mustard (there is no sugar in regular mustard), ¼ cup honey, 2-3 Tablespoons cider vinegar and 2 Tablespoons vegetable oil. Add a little salt and whisk well. Drizzle this over the salad. Delicious!

Cashew Salad

1 cup salted cashews
¾ c slivered almonds
½ cup sunflower kernels
6 green onions, chopped
1 head Nappa cabbage, chopped fine

Sauté the nuts and sunflower kernels in a tiny amount of olive oil just until barely browned. Add to the cabbage and onions and top with Oil & Vinegar dressing.

17 THE GOOD, THE BAD & THE UGLY

Ahab, King of Samaria, was not one of the nicest people in the world back in the day. As a matter of fact, only one person was known to be WORSE than 'ole King Ahab and that was his wife, whose name has since become synonymous with a manipulative, controlling, and even wicked individual. Maybe you have heard it said that one has a *Jezebel spirit*. It is not a compliment!

King Ahab married Jezebel out of the will of God and relinquished his power as king to her. (1 Kings 1)

Their roles were reversed from the *get-go* and it spelled disaster.

Ahab came home one day upset because there was a beautiful vineyard that he wanted to have next to the palace but he could not because it was owned by a man named Naboth. He wanted to keep it in his family and did not wish to sell. Ahab offered him a very fair price but still Naboth declined. Ahab became so upset that he would not eat.

Jezebel was furious with Ahab for his weak ways and declared that the vineyard would be his (or better yet, hers). She began to plot her plan.

She wrote letters to the elders and the nobles and saying, *"Proclaim a fast, and set Naboth on high among the people: And set two men, sons of Belial, before him, to bear witness against him, saying, Thou didst blaspheme God and the king. And then carry him out, and stone him, that he may die."* 1 Kings 21:9-10.

Naturally her minions followed her instructions and Naboth was killed. But did you catch what has happened here?

Jezebel has proclaimed a fast!

Obviously religion was the furthest thing from her mind, or Ahab's either. But in order to make it all look good, she must order the fast, as if to appear that either a threat had been made on Ahab's life or a calamity was coming upon the kingdom.

She sat Naboth *"on high among the people"*, not necessarily as the guilty one, but because of his high honor in the community. Then, when the two men that had been *planted* to tell lies against him started their stories, Naboth was seated up where the guilty usually sat, where everyone could see him.

It worked; just as she had planned. He was convicted, and stoned to death.

When Ahab heard that Naboth was dead, he hurried down to take possession of the vineyard. News traveled fast because the Lord also told Elijah…

> *"Arise, go down to meet Ahab king of Israel, which is in Samaria: behold, he is in the vineyard of Naboth, whither he is gone down to possess it. And thou shalt speak unto him, saying, Thus saith the Lord, Hast thou killed, and also taken possession? …In the place where dogs licked the blood of Naboth shall dogs lick thy blood, even thine."* 1 Kings 21:18-19 KJV.

But that wasn't all. Elijah had much to say to Ahab that day and began to tell him of all his wicked ways and how he was about to come face to face with judgment for the evil life that he had lived. His time was up!

You just don't play around with the things of God and get by with it forever. There are consequences for sin. Sometimes it is in this life, sometimes it is not until Judgment, but there are consequences.

Fasting and prayer are effective, life-changing, powerful ways to see things happen in the spirit world.

But God does not honor efforts that are used against others for harm and evil influence, like we have seen here with Jezebel!

God was letting Ahab know there were to be consequences for the actions of his wife and that Ahab was just as guilty of murder as if he had pulled the trigger.

"But there was none like unto Ahab, which did sell himself to work wickedness in the sight of the Lord, whom Jezebel his wife stirred up." 1 Kings 21:25 KJV The New Living Translation says, *"No one else so completely sold himself to what was evil in the LORD's sight as Ahab did under the influence of his wife Jezebel."*

But something must have struck a chord in Ahab for the Bible tells us that he was listening to the prophet Elijah.

"And it came to pass, when Ahab heard those words, that he rent his clothes, and put sackcloth upon his flesh, and fasted, and lay in sackcloth, and went softly." 1 Kings 21:27 KJV.

He was fasting again. Not because Jezebel had told him to. Not because he was trying to deceive anyone and not because he was trying to murder anyone.

"And the word of the Lord came to Elijah the Tishbite, saying, Seest thou how Ahab humbleth himself before me? Because he humbleth himself before me, I will not bring the evil in his days: but in his son's days will I bring the evil upon his house." 1 Kings 21:28-29 KJV.

He was fasting because he was broken, scared and humbled.

And the Lord said because he *HUMBLED* himself he spared Ahab the *judgment* in *HIS* days. Jezebel still came to an untimely end as promised. She doesn't humble herself one bit as far as the scriptures tell us. But Ahab had learned his lesson for now.

There are fasts that are *NOT* pleasing to God.

- Fasts that are only to be seen of men.
- Fasts that make us look good or holy.
- Fasts that are just to make us lose weight; we call those diets! *(Of course we know if you lose weight from fasting, that is another matter entirely. We have had testimonies of lives changed permanently through fasting for their health. Our lives SHOULD be changed from fasting!)*

Fasts are also not to be used against others. Sounds ridiculous to even say it, but Jezebel tried it.

The fast that works is the kind that is coupled with prayer, humility and brokenness. A fast should keep you on your knees and searching for more time with the Savior. Clean out the old and allow God to fill you up with more and more of His spirit.

Changing the inside!

Nothing is too hard for God. If he can humble a man like Ahab, there is hope for all of us!

Let our fasting be done with humility of heart and for the right purpose: to draw closer to Him, to reach for others and to seek the perfect will of God for our lives.

RECIPES

Baked Apples

2 cups sliced apples, unpeeled
1 cup unsweetened apple juice
Sprinkle of cinnamon

Preheat oven to 350 degrees. Place sliced apples in an 8x8 inch baking dish. Whisk the cinnamon into the apple juice. Pour over the apples. Bake for 15 minutes, stir and bake for another 15 minutes. Serve warm. *Four servings, about ½ cup each.*

Serve over baked oatmeal or brown rice. Sprinkle the top with unsweetened coconut or chopped pecans.

Chips & Salsa

These are so good and so good for you! They are nothing like what you get in a restaurant or a bag. All you need are whole wheat tortillas. Use a pizza cutter and cut each tortilla into four triangles. Spread on a baking sheet in a single layer, not touching, and bake 8-10 minutes at 400 degrees. You can sprinkle a little bit of salt before baking for extra flavor or cayenne pepper to make them a bit spicy. Get creative.

Salsa

1 onion, chopped,
2 green peppers, chopped
1 red pepper, chopped
5-6 Roma tomatoes diced
1 jalapeno chopped and seeded
1 garlic clove minced
Cilantro, sea salt and a squeeze of lime juice.

Mix together well, let sit and allow flavors to come together.

18 THE BATTLE IS NOT YOURS, BUT GOD'S!

Jehoshaphat didn't waste any time when he found out that Judah was about to be attacked. He did what any smart man of God would have done. Any king that knew of the God of Abraham, Isaac and Jacob would call a fast! Not just any fast, but all of Judah came together to pray and seek their God for His help.

The end of their prayer for help went like this: *"O our God, wilt thou not judge them? For we have no might against this great company that cometh against us; neither know we what to do: but our eyes are upon thee."* 2 Chronicles 20:12 KJV.

They came together in unity, with their wives, their children, the Bible even says *"...with their little ones."*

Then something powerful happened. Jahaziel was standing there with the rest of them when suddenly the Spirit of the Lord came upon him and he said, *"...Thus saith the LORD unto you, Be not afraid nor dismayed by reason of this great multitude; for the battle is not yours, but God's...Tomorrow go ye down against them...and ye shall find them at the end of the brook...**Ye shall not need to fight*** *in this battle: set yourselves, stand ye still, and see the salvation of the* **LORD** *with you,* *O Judah and Jerusalem: fear not, nor be dismayed; tomorrow go out against them: for the LORD will be with you."* 2 Chronicles 20:15-17 KJV.

What an answer to prayer!

What power!

What authority!

The next morning they got up early and headed into the wilderness and King Jehoshaphat said, *"Believe in the LORD your God, so shall ye be established; believe his prophets, so shall ye prosper."* 2 Chronicles 20:20 KJV.

I love what he does next. He appointed singers, *"...unto the LORD, just to praise the beauty of holiness, and as they went out before the army, just to say, Praise the LORD; for his mercy endureth for ever."* Wow!

They took time to praise the LORD in the MIDDLE of the battle!

So what did they do since they didn't have to fight? They worshipped and gave Him the praise that He deserved.

They had fasted; they had prayed.

He had heard; He had answered.

Now they were giving Him back the praise because He was worthy! When they began to sing and praise, then the LORD began to act. The Bible says He set an ambush against the Ammonites, Moabites and Mount Seir and they were all *smitten!*

Why did the children of Judah not have to fight? The children of Ammon and Moab stood up against the inhabitants of Mount Seir, trying to destroy them. So when they had accomplished that *then they destroyed one another!*

When Judah showed up at the watch tower in the wilderness they looked out at the multitude and all they could see were the dead, *"none escaped."*

"And the fear of God was on all the kingdoms of those countries, when they had heard that the LORD fought against the enemies of Israel."

Good news travels fast. Bad news travels fast. God had delivered His people once again because they trusted in Him.

What can you believe God for today? What are you needing an answer for in your life? What battles are you trying to fight on your own?

Stand still and see the salvation of the Lord!

He is your VICTORIOUS WARRIOR and this is HIS BATTLE, not yours! Let Him take care of it for you. Trust Him, put your confidence in Him and then do what King Jehoshaphat and his people did...

Worship and give Him praise for the victory that is coming! Whether you see it today or tomorrow doesn't matter. He is in control and His timing is perfect. Trust Him for the victory and then rest in His promises.

Praise gives strength and victory then the walls will come down!

RECIPES

Another Daniel Fast BREAKFAST idea! **Brown Rice Cakes** with All Natural Peanut Butter and All Fruit Spread (no sugar added).

Bring back **Cream of Wheat**! Toss in some berries or bananas, unsweetened almond or soy milk and if you are using raw honey, just a drop and you have a hot, delicious, Daniel Fast approved breakfast.

I hope you enjoy these recipes and the Lord is giving you strength on your journey!

19 LOOKING FOR THE REDEMPTION

"And there was one Anna, a prophetess…she was of a great age, and had lived with an husband seven years from her virginity; And she was a widow of about fourscore and four years, which departed not from the temple, but served God with fastings and prayers night and day." Luke 2:36-37.

The story of Anna, the prophetess, as found in the Gospel of Luke, is fascinating on so many levels. Let me introduce this amazing lady to you…

Anna was old. The Bible tells us she had been married for seven years and then widowed. It is a little difficult to decipher whether she had been a widow for 84 years or she was 84 years old when we encounter her in Luke 2.

If it is the former, then she was around 105, which would not be out of the question, and many scholars agree this could be the case. She could have married at 14, a very common age to have married in those days, became a widow at 21, and then we come upon her at the temple 84 years later, at the ripe old age of 105.

This lovely lady served in the temple, night and day!

The Word even tells us she doesn't leave. She is the only woman mentioned by name in the New Testament as being a prophetess. (*Philip's daughters are said to have prophesied in Acts 21:9.*) She is highly honored in this regard as someone who can touch the throne of heaven with her prayers.

What is her significance here today?

Joseph and Mary had brought Jesus to Jerusalem to *"...present him to the Lord..."* Luke 2:22. As was their custom, every Jewish male baby had to be brought to the temple and a sacrifice made to the Lord: a pair of turtledoves or two young pigeons.

The parents of Jesus first encountered Simeon when they arrive at the temple. *"And, behold, there was a man in Jerusalem, whose name was Simeon; and the same man was just and devout, waiting for the consolation of Israel: and the Holy Ghost was upon him."*

"Waiting for the consolation of Israel." What does that mean?

The same word used here for consolation is the same word Jesus used later when He described the Holy Spirit as the *Comforter*. The word is *paraklesis* and it means *"...one who comes alongside to help, one who pleads a cause..."*

So Simeon was waiting for the Comforter!

He was waiting for the Messiah. When Mary and Joseph handed the child, Jesus, to him the Bible says, *"Then took he him up in his arms, and blessed God, and said, Lord, now lettest thou thy servant depart in peace, according to thy word: For mine eyes have seen thy salvation, Which thou hast prepared before the face of all people; A light to lighten the Gentiles, and the glory of thy people Israel."*

The Comforter, the Consolation, the Messiah, had come!

As far as Simeon was concerned, he could die in peace. What he had been working for, waiting for and living his entire life telling others about, had finally arrived.

Then they encountered Anna, who had spent her time much like Simeon, fasting, praying and telling everyone she could about the One who was to come. She saw Joseph, Mary and Jesus with Simeon and this is what the Bible had to say about their meeting:

> *"And she coming in that instant gave thanks likewise unto the Lord, and spake of him to all them that looked for redemption in Jerusalem."* Luke 2:38 KJV.

Look closely, or you will miss it. She comes up. She was not introduced. But immediately, in that instant, she gave thanks, and began to give God praise. She didn't hesitate for one moment to tell everyone there that this was the *REDEMPTION of Jerusalem!*

How did Anna know? Because she fasted; she prayed daily. She spent time with God, she knew Him and she was waiting for the promise.

She recognized Him when He came.

Will you know Him?

Will you recognize Him in an instant?

Like Anna, we must spend our days in relationship with Jesus Christ. We cannot afford any less than to love Him, to delve deep into the Word and into prayer and fasting. We must deny our flesh the pleasures of this world and realize that these things will pass away. We will not be taking them with us!

Only what is done for Christ will last. Only reaching for the lost will be what really matters in the end. We will be so glad we spent our time on things eternal.

Reach out to Him today…He is waiting for you!

RECIPES

Brown Rice with Cashews

Heat 1 teaspoon olive oil in pan; lightly brown ¼ cup drained crushed pineapple *(no syrup)*; stir in ¾ cup cooked brown rice, 2 Tablespoons chopped cashews. Add 1½ cup steamed broccoli or snow peas for extra veggies!

Rice & Beans, Mexican Variety

1 Tablespoon olive oil
1 cup diced red onions
1 cloves garlic, minced
2 ½ cups water
1 ½ cups brown rice, uncooked
1 (10-oz.) can diced tomatoes and green chilies
1 teaspoon cumin
¼ teaspoon cayenne pepper
1 (15.5-oz.) can black beans, rinsed and drained
1 Tablespoon chopped fresh parsley or 1 teaspoon dried parsley

Start by rinsing the rice in a strainer under cold water, about 30 seconds. Drain. Heat olive oil over medium heat then add onions and cook five minutes. Add the garlic, cook another minute. Add the water, tomatoes, rice, chilies, cayenne pepper and cumin. Bring to boil. Reduce the heat, cover then simmer for about 45 minutes. Be sure and check to see if rice is tender and the liquid is absorbed. Then add the beans and mix well. Cook about 8-10 minutes, add parsley if desired, serve. *Makes about six servings; one cup each.* This is a little spicy! You could eliminate the cayenne pepper or cut it down some.

20 FACE TO FACE

"And the LORD spake unto Moses face to face, as a man speaketh unto his friend." Exodus 33:11 KJV.

"And the LORD descended in the cloud, and stood with him there, and proclaimed the name of the LORD. And the LORD passed by before him, and proclaimed, The LORD, The LORD God, merciful and gracious, longsuffering, and abundant in goodness and truth, Keeping mercy for thousands, forgiving iniquity and transgression and sin..." Exodus 34:5-7 KJV.

Poor Moses. He couldn't leave his **congregation** for any matter of time before they were breaking all the rules.

As soon as they would get themselves in trouble, the Lord would want to punish them, or even wipe them off the planet, and Moses would *"stand in the gap"*, intercede and literally beg for God to give them another chance.

So there he was on the Mount a second time, he had already broken the Tablets containing the Ten Commandments the first time God had handwritten them. He was back up there alone. Joshua is waiting a few hundred feet down the mountain and Aaron is in charge back at home.

"And he was there with the LORD forty days and forty nights; he did neither eat bread, nor drink water. And he wrote upon the tables the words of the covenant, the ten commandments." Exodus 34:28 KJV.

Forty days and forty nights!

The results of the fast show the effects it was having on Moses. *"And it came to pass, when Moses came down from mount Sinai with the two tables of testimony in Moses' hand, when he came down from the mount, that Moses wist not that the skin of his face shone while he talked with him."* Exodus 34:29 KJV.

His face was shining with the glory of God! That was not just the result of **seeing God** because the Bible says that the nobles and the elders also saw God in some form or fashion when they all first went up on the Mount. (Exodus 24:9-11)

The people could not even stand to look at Moses because of the glory of God. He had to keep a veil on his face when he spoke to the people and he could only take it off when he went into the temple to minister to the Lord. *"When Moses finished speaking with them, he covered his face with a veil."* Exodus 34:33 NLT.

What do I look like after I have been with God?

What do people see after I have spent time with the Savior?

Is there a difference in me; is there a light on my face from the glory of God?

Should there be?

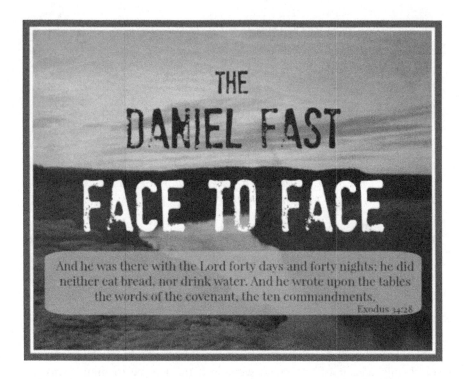

Yet again, shouldn't there be something about us that will draw others to us and point them to Christ? *And if it isn't the fact that we have been in HIS PRESENCE, then what is it?*

Fasting, praying and spending time in His Word is what will continually build a relationship with the Savior and will radiate His glory.

They will also notice it if we **DON'T** do it.

We might not actually see God face to face, but we can spend time with Him every day, in His glory, in His presence. We can have the spirit of God, the Holy Ghost, dwelling IN us, with us, ALIVE!

Let us be like Moses. Fasting and praying on a regular basis is definitely good Christian character-building.

We can give back by giving our lives as a sacrifice, wholly consecrated and fully devoted, reaching for the lost and living full of joy and hope and watching for His return.

RECIPES

Fruit & Nut Bars

1 ½ cup almonds
1 ½ cup raisins
1 ¼ teaspoon cinnamon

Rinse the raisins and almonds with water. Toss them in a food processor with the cinnamon. Whirl away! When sufficiently mixed, form into ball or bar shapes. *Makes about 12 small balls or 6 large bars.*

Beautiful Green Salad

6-8 cups baby spinach
1 cucumber, cut into chunks
1 sweet orange, sliced into sections or triangles
½ medium red onion, sliced into rings
1 cup roasted sliced almonds
1½ cup dried cranberries
1½ cup balsamic vinaigrette salad dressing

Place spinach onto salad plates. Top with red onion, cucumber chunks, orange slices, cranberries and sliced almonds. Add the dressing and serve.

21 FOR ALL THE RIGHT REASONS

"For if thou altogether holdest thy peace at this time, then shall there enlargement and deliverance arise to the Jews from another place; but thou and thy father's house shall be destroyed: and who knoweth whether thou art come to the kingdom for such a time as this?" Esther 4:14 KJV.

Ah, Esther.

She is complicated.

If you are familiar with the story of Esther and her cousin, Mordecai (Esther 2:7), you are aware that she was just an average young lady enjoying her normal life until Queen Vashti was kicked out of the palace for *rebellion* against the king. A new queen had to be found and Esther's beauty landed her the part.

Soon, Mordecai overheard a plot by Haman, a man who was *above all the princes* in the king's court, to destroy the Jewish people. Mordecai realized that Esther was the only hope they had of getting to the king and having the decree abolished.

Esther called for a fast.

We are all aware that the book of Esther never mentions God, no reference to Him, nothing whatsoever about Jehovah in the entire book. We *assume* they are serving Him, fasting to get His attention and praying along with the fasting.

But it is never mentioned.

I have always found that intriguing when the rest of the Bible is so full of the Almighty. Let us step outside of tradition, from what we have always been taught in Sunday School, and look at this story with a different set of eyes.

Why doesn't Esther ever call on the Lord for help? Why doesn't Mordecai refer to Him in any of his pleas to Esther? Where do they think their help is going to come from?

We assume there was repentance; we assume there was prayer with the fasting because that is what we read with all of the other accounts in the Bible. But it is absent in this story.

Maybe the story of Esther is more of a lesson in what fasting is NOT because it cannot be absent in our story.

They had all of the right actions, the right motions, but they didn't know God.

They didn't talk ABOUT Him, and they didn't talk WITH Him!

Yes, the Jewish people were spared from Haman's despicable plan and he was destroyed in their place. God was protecting His chosen people. Esther and Mordecai could be called heroes for their brave actions to step in and put their lives on the line for the Jewish nation.

But we need to be careful when we fast that we do it for the right reasons, with a right spirit and a clean heart.

Fasting without prayer is just going without food. It has no spiritual benefits and will yield no spiritual fruit.

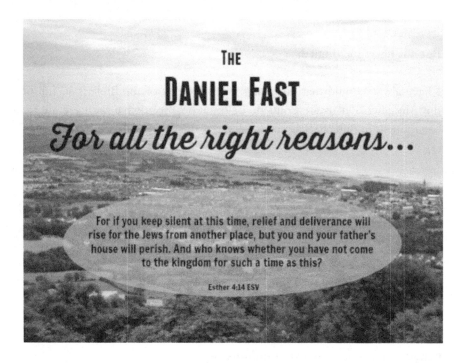

Mordecai's famous line, *"...who knoweth whether thou art come to the kingdom for such a time as this?"* is a great example to us today. Truly, Esther was put in that position to be able to stand in the gap for the Jewish people. But whether she and her cousin Mordecai were godly people or not remains to be seen.

What will others say about us? That we did all of the right things but didn't know Jesus? What will the Lord say about us? He warns in the New Testament of that very thing when the people begin to list all of the things they had done in His name. His reply? *"And then will I profess unto them, I never knew you: depart from me, ye that work iniquity."* Matthew 7:23 KJV.

Let's make sure as we close out our Daniel Fasts that this is not our *last* fast!

We need to make fasting a regular part of our spiritual discipline; we will only become stronger and closer to the One who intervenes for us in our crisis situations!

RECIPE

Veggie Tacos

1 large sweet potato, cubed
2½ cups spinach, fresh
¼ red onion, sliced very thin
1½ Tablespoon olive oil
½ teaspoon paprika
½ teaspoon chili powder
Salt and Pepper
¼ teaspoon oregano
Juice from one lime
½ avocado, mashed *(optional)*

Toss the sweet potato with all of the spices. Add the sweet potatoes to heated oil and cook for 10-15 minutes until tender. Add spinach and cook about three minutes, until wilted. Serve in warm whole wheat tortillas with lime juice. You may also like adding the mashed avocado to your tortillas as a spread!

22 EBENEZER! THE LORD HAS HELPED US

I hope you are encouraged by Ebenezer. Have you never heard of him? That's alright; in this story Ebenezer is not a him. Let's look at the story.

Israel was in trouble again. They had been without the Ark of the Covenant for 20 years and were fairly content to let it sit at the house of Abinadab. No one wanted to risk the fate of those returning the ark of the Lord for on that day 50,070 people in Betheshemesh were struck down for *looking at the ark*!

Israel is grieved that the Ark is sitting in the house of Abinadab, *"...and all the house of Israel lamented after the Lord."* 1 Samuel 7:2 KJV.

Samuel came to the people with an answer: *"And Samuel said to all the house of Israel, 'If you are returning to the LORD with all your heart, then put away the foreign gods and the Ashtaroth from among you and direct your heart to the LORD and serve him only, and he will deliver you out of the hand of the Philistines.'"* 1 Samuel 7:3, 4 ESV.

The Bible says they did just that. They put away the gods of Baalim and Ashteroth and served the Lord **ONLY**.

Samuel then told them to gather at Mizpeh where he would pray for them. *"And they gathered together to Mizpeh, and drew water, and poured it out before the Lord, and fasted on that day, and said there, 'We have sinned against the Lord.' And Samuel judged the children of Israel in Mizpeh."* 1 Samuel 7:6.

The pouring out of water is not completely clear. It could be the washing away of guilt, repentance, or even self-denial. Obviously they were coming together in some form of unity to show they were sorrowful and turning back to God.

Then they **fasted the entire day** and confessed that they had sinned against the Lord. It says Samuel judged them, but he was also their leader, their mentor, guide and **shepherd**. When they sinned, he let them know they had committed wrong and needed correction.

Here they are gathered together confessing, repenting and asking God to forgive them of their sins so they can be delivered completely from the Philistines. Guess who shows up?

The Philistines heard that the Israelites had *gathered together* so they *gather together* to go up against them. Then the Israelites *heard that* the Philistines *had heard* that the Israelites had *gathered together* and now the Philistines were coming up against the Israelites and they were terrified!

The children of Israel cried out to Samuel, *"And the children of Israel said to Samuel, Cease not to cry unto the Lord our God for us, that he will save us out of the hand of the Philistines."* 1 Samuel 7:8 KJV.

In other words, "Don't stop praying now, Samuel. *HELP us!*"

Samuel offered a burnt offering to the Lord, *"...and the Lord heard him."* 1 Samuel 7:9 KJV.

THE DANIEL FAST

Come on people! You already repented; you had turned from your wicked ways by putting away your false gods and had served God ONLY, the Word says. You were fasting, praying, (or Samuel was praying *for* you), and when trouble showed up, panic set in.

Does it sound familiar? We repent, we pray, we fast, we pour ourselves into the Word but then when trouble comes, *we panic.* "HELP!"

We stumble; we fall and think our mustard seed faith needs a little *plant food* to get it growing again.

Or does it?

"And as Samuel was offering up the burnt offering, the Philistines drew near to battle against Israel: but the Lord thundered with a great thunder on that day upon the Philistines, and discomfited them; and they were smitten before Israel." 1 Samuel 7:10 KJV.

Discomfited them means that the Lord confused them to the point where the Israelites could overcome them and win the battle!

Doesn't He do the same for us today? When we call on the Name of Jesus, our enemies are confused; they have to flee. There is power in that Name! When we act on the authority that we have as a child of the King, all of the enemies of this world have to take notice of us.

WE have authority! *"...greater is he that is in us than he that is in the world!"* 1 John 4:4 KJV.

And here is my favorite part:

"Then Samuel took a stone, and set it between Mizpeh and Shen, and called the name of it Ebenezer, saying, Hitherto hath the Lord helped us." 1 Samuel 7:12 KJV.

Ebenezer...up until now the Lord has helped us.

But wait, it gets better.

"So the Philistines were subdued, and they came no more into the coast of Israel: and the hand of the Lord was against the Philistines all the days of Samuel." 1 Samuel 7:13 KJV.

They did not come any more into the coast of Israel! The hand of the Lord was against the Philistines ALL THE DAYS of Samuel!

Samuel was honored by the Lord with protection the rest of his days.

Why?

Samuel honored the Lord with his prayers, his fasting, his teachings, and with his ***LIFE***.

Wouldn't it be great if the same could be said of us today?

Ebenezer, up until now the Lord has helped us. What a mighty testimony. But it will not stop there.

"All the days of _____." Fill in your name!

God is fighting for you, He is with you, and He is faithful and true. We can trust His promises just as Samuel did all of those many, many years ago.

Be blessed with hope!

RECIPES

Zucchini Fries

1 medium zucchini
½ cup cornmeal
½ teaspoon garlic salt
½ teaspoon chili powder
¼ teaspoon each paprika and cumin
Pepper
1½ cup water
Olive oil

Preheat oven to 350 degrees. Lightly grease a cookie sheet and set aside. Mix together cornmeal, chili powder, cumin, paprika, pepper and garlic salt.

Slice zucchini into strips about three inches long. Dip each strip in water and dredge in cornmeal mixture, coating well. Place about 1-inch apart on cookie sheet and then *spray the zucchini* with cooking oil. Bake in preheated oven for about 20-25 minutes.

23 EZRA. BY THE GOOD HAND OF GOD

Ezra. Some thought he had nothing to say. He was one of those who did so much for his *present world* but yet his mind was clearly on the one to come!

The seventh chapter of the book bearing his name tells us right away what kind of man he was: *"This Ezra went up from Babylon; and he was a ready scribe in the law of Moses, which the Lord God of Israel had given: and the king granted him all his request, according to the hand of the Lord his God upon him."* Ezra 7:6 KJV.

Ezra's lineage was traced all the way back to Aaron, the brother of Moses. He was a teacher, a *soper*, translated as a *scribe, a writer, recorder or secretary*. It also meant that he could obviously read and write; he was a learned man who could teach what he read in the Law of God.

He had favor with the pagan ruler, King Artaxerxes, and the king was willing to grant him whatever was requested of him.

So what was Ezra's request? Jewels? Land? Power?

No.

Ezra didn't choose any of these; he chose to take some of the people of God back to Jerusalem. *"For Ezra had prepared his heart to seek the law of the Lord, and to do it, and to teach in Israel statutes and judgments."* Ezra 7:10 KJV.

The King gave a letter to Ezra outlining how all of this was to take place. The trip was to take four months. They were to have certain *privileges* along the way. The king gave them plenty of gold and silver for their journey and they were to stop and get more in Babylon.

Check this out: They were carrying 3.5. tons of silver, 600 bushels of wheat, 600 gallons of wine, 100 baths of olive oil, and an unlimited salt supply. This was not to be a poor caravan traveling through the desert; these people were going in style!

How did King Artaxerxes benefit from all of this generosity? He hoped to have peace with his neighbors *"…for why should we risk bringing God's anger against the realm of the king and his sons?"* Ezra 7:23 NKJV.

Ezra was busy gathering the people for the trip and then he asked God for His blessing on the journey. Ezra's character and true spirit come out here in this prayer.

"Then I proclaimed a fast there at the river of Ahava, that we might humble ourselves before our God, to seek from Him the right way for us and our little ones and all our possessions." Ezra 8:21 NKJV.

Ezra wanted the people to humble themselves. The King James Version says to *afflict*, to repent, to show dependence on their God for the huge expedition they were about to embark upon. Ezra realized without God's help they would be subject to thieves because they were carrying so much gold and other treasures.

But what he said next is amazing. *"For I was ashamed to request of the king an escort of soldiers and horsemen to help us against the enemy on the road, because we had spoken to the king, saying, 'The hand of our God is upon all those for good who seek Him, but His power and His wrath are against all those who forsake Him.' So we fasted and entreated our God for this, and He answered our prayer."* Ezra 8:22, 23 NKJV.

He could have asked for a military escort because of all he was carrying but Ezra didn't want to do that since he had already told the king that the hand of God was on them. Now he had to act on that faith.

Everything Ezra taught, everything he said, and now everything he believed, was being put into action.

So he did what he needed to do. He humbled himself, and made the people do the same. They fasted and *entreated God*, or prayed and asked God for help! Ezra knew that this God that he had put his faith and confidence in, this God that he had trusted and read about, wrote about and taught about continually, would be faithful. He was not disappointed for the Bible says,

"...and He answered our prayer."

What need do you have today?

Is there something you have been struggling to even *ask* God about?

Is it His protection you wish?

Do you need His wisdom for a particular situation?

What about mercy? Are you struggling to give it where it is needed?

You don't have to worry, fret and wring your hands in despair!

Trust as Ezra did, he lived for His God; he didn't just talk about Him, he *knew* Him!

So when trouble came his way, or doubt tried to creep in, uncertainty or even *thieves* lurked nearby, he knew exactly what to do.

He humbled his soul with fasting, he prayed for God's protection and then...

He stepped out in faith!

He arrived safely at his destination. He never lost any of the 25 tons of silver, silver articles weighing 3.75, tons, 3.75 tons of gold, 20 huge bowls of gold, all which would have been worth millions of dollars today. All of the people could now worship their God in their homeland. Once again, Jehovah had protected them from harm.

So walk in victory today. God is on your side! You can trust Him to be faithful when you live for Him and put Him first.

> *"And the hand of our God was upon us, and He delivered us from the hand of the enemy..."* Ezra 8:31 NKJV.

RECIPE

Corn Chowder

½ Tablespoon olive oil
½ cup diced onion
4 cups water
1 pound potatoes, peeled and diced (about 3 cups)
1 clove garlic, minced
1 teaspoon dried parsley flakes
½ teaspoon salt
Pepper
3½ cups fresh or frozen corn kernels
½ cups unsweetened almond milk

Heat olive oil in a large pan; add onions. Cook until translucent. Add water, potatoes, garlic, parsley, salt, and pepper. Bring to a boil. Reduce heat and simmer, covered, 15-20 minutes or until potatoes are tender. Add corn and almond milk. Cook uncovered, over low heat for another 10 minutes. Place 3 cups of soup in a food processor or blender, and process about 15 seconds. Return to saucepan. Stir well, and serve.

Tomorrow is your last day!

24 LIVES WERE CHANGED; PRAYERS WERE ANSWERED

You did it! Even if you were tempted to cheat, accidentally forgot, or even purposely went off of the fast and back on again, you have accomplished something amazing. Do not beat yourself up if you weren't perfect during the fast. You will be more diligent as you continue to make *fasting* a regular part of your spiritual and physical lifestyle.

Fasting has so many health benefits. Some studies show it is effective against cancer; it could also reduce the risk of developing cancer, guard against diabetes and heart disease, help control asthma and even help ward off Parkinson's disease and dementia.

We do not take the best care of ourselves with our hectic lifestyles and eat-on-the-run schedules. Regular fasting will detox your body and get rid of poisons. It gives your digestive system a much needed rest. It will reduce your blood sugar, which will in turn break down fat. It can even correct high blood pressure and will definitely improve your immunity.

There are *spiritual benefits* that are out of this world!

Has the Lord spoken to your heart during the fast?

Have prayers been answered?

Do you feel as if you have drawn closer to the Savior?

Even if you started your fast for a particular reason, and still do not see an answer, do not despair. God will answer at just the right time, always ON time.

Fasting is never wasted before the Lord if it is done for the right reasons. We have mentioned many times that it is so much more than just going without food. If that is all you are doing then it truly was just a diet program.

But when you are desperate for a move of God in your life, fasting will help bring those results!

Fasting helps move everything else out of the way so you can hear HIS voice more clearly. *"Blessed are they which do hunger and thirst after righteousness: for they shall be filled."* Matthew 5:6 KJV.

Fasting will break strongholds in the demonic world! *"And he said unto them, 'This kind can come forth by nothing, but by prayer and fasting.'"* Mark 9:29 KJV.

The disciples could not cast the evil spirit out and had to get Jesus to help. That is when He told them it would take prayer *AND* fasting.

The prophet Daniel found out how real it was when the angel showed up to meet with him after his 21 day fast: *"Fear not, Daniel: for from the first day that thou didst set thine heart to understand, and to chasten thyself before thy God, thy words were heard, and I am come for thy words. But the prince of the kingdom of Persia withstood me one and twenty days: but, lo, Michael, one of the chief princes, came to help me; and I remained there with the kings of Persia."* Daniel 10:12-13 KJV.

Fasting will definitely strengthen your prayer life. It will help you *die out* to the flesh and be sensitive to the power of the Holy Spirit.

I pray this devotional has been a blessing to you, no matter how often, how many days or which way you chose to fast. And I hope **WE ALL** will continue to draw closer to the Lord through regular fasting and prayer.

RECIPES

Potato Zucchini Casserole

1 pound potatoes, *unpeeled* and cut into ½-inch cubes
1 cup fresh corn kernels (about 2 ears)
1 cup thinly-sliced green onion
2 cups chopped zucchini, unpeeled
1 clove garlic, minced
2 tablespoons olive oil, divided
½ fresh basil
½ teaspoon salt

Dash of pepper

Preheat oven to 425 degrees. Mix potatoes and corn in a large bowl. Add 1 Tablespoon olive oil, basil, salt, and pepper. Stir. Place on an 11x17-inch baking sheet. Bake about 25 minutes or until potatoes are tender, stirring halfway through cooking time.

About five minutes before potatoes are finished, heat 1 Tablespoon olive oil on stovetop and add onion slices and zucchini. Stir fry until slightly browned. Add garlic and cook about 30 seconds. Add potatoes and corn. Stir well, and cook another 5 minutes before serving.

ABOUT THE AUTHOR

Nannette Elkins has served in various ministry positions, most recently as a pastor's wife and missionary to Northern Europe serving in the countries of Estonia and Latvia.

An aspiring writer, speaker, teacher and editor, she was kicked out of her comfort zone by God and enjoys encouraging others through her blog, HopeintheHealing.com and monthly at Internet Café Devotions.

She travels with her husband as the North America Directors for **Revival By Design (rbdna.org)**, helping churches prepare for end-time revival from a Bible-based blueprint.

Attached to The Sweetheart for 35 years, she is finding contentment in their empty nest and the delightful chaos of working for God. The joys of her life, Kyle, Rachel, Kristopher and Korey Ross, remind her that she has accomplished a few good things in this life.

Nannette Elkins

Made in the USA
Las Vegas, NV
11 January 2024

84233621R00075